D1080650

Parisian
bistros
THE GUIDE

Warning

Do you know what restaurant life is like? Just like yours, it's busy and boisterous. Restaurants open up, they close, they change chefs, revolutionize their menus and raise their prices. *C'est la vie*. That's the reason why, even though we were extra-careful to check every single address in this book when we wrote it, we can't guarantee that all of the information given here will still be relevant when you go looking for the perfect bistro. That's life, and we love it just as it is...

Parisian bistros
THE GUIDE

Thierry Richard – Amélie Weill

Photographs: **Juliette Ranck**
Illustrations: **Aseyn**

CHÊNE

~ Contents ~

— *Foreword* —
OUR OWN BISTRO

Thierry Richard & Amélie Weill

Parisian bistros. What a subject! That magic word conjures up images, memories, hungers, and is enough to give us an appetite by itself! In this book we wanted to find, uncover, and share the details of the very best Parisian bistros – places where we love to hang out with friends and eat lunch or dinner without any fuss. Places that don't necessarily aim to be *à la mode* or trendy (although some of them are), but that celebrate authenticity and human warmth. Didn't we say it was quite a subject?

"Please, mister – draw me a bistro!" Bistros are an ambitious subject because they call out to people's experiences, habits, and tastes. The bistro reflects its customers' soul, their stomach, and their memory.

So what exactly is a bistro in this guide? What's the difference between a bistro and a restaurant, or a brasserie? My God, all of this is so subjective! For us, bistros (at least, the ones you'll find in these pages) are first and foremost congenial places where friends love to meet up and share real, simple food, to truly live in the present, or to sense the atmosphere of the past. Places where the proprietor brings the room to life, where everyone knows their waiter's name. What we love in a bistro is the vibrant life that surrounds the plate. A Claude Sautet scene. A bistro can overlap with a brasserie or a local café; it can be as chic as a restaurant or welcome Parisian street urchins; it might have been born yesterday or have existed in Paris for years. They are simply frank, sincere, heartfelt, and they stay true to their initial mission: to feed their customers with good food and good feelings.

Here are a few guidelines that helped us put this book together. A bistro is:
- A place where the chef is in the kitchen every day, not parading around a palace in southeast Asia every other week
- A place that takes bookings
- A place where you can choose what you want to eat
- A place where the food is neither pretentious nor gourmet, but simple, sincere, fresh, and prepared entirely on the spot
- A place where human generosity warms hearts on cold winter nights, and freshens them on hot summer days

In other words, a bistro is a place that looks after other people before taking care of itself.

We can already hear you saying: "But why didn't you include that one or this one? I just love their celeriac remoulade!" And, of course, while reading through these pages, you will inevitably think "this one is missing" or "that one is more of a brasserie, isn't it?" Well, maybe. And so what?

This selection is ours, it is free, and we take full responsibility for it. It was voluntarily whittled down to the 100 best places (isn't that enough?), that we all love for different reasons, explained throughout the book.

So, follow us! Read through these pages, try these places, trust our enthusiasm for returning bourgeois cuisine back to its full glory, to leeks vinaigrette and veal *blanquette*. Hop onto the land of checkered napkins (or not), Laguiole knives (or not), bring your healthy appetite, and join us at the table. We're already waiting for you there with a drink...

THE ESSENTIALS

This is the most debatable chapter in this book. Here, subjectivity reigns supreme, and our usual professionalism and care have given way to our bad faith. These are our own, very personal favorites. Our best of the best, among the best – that's to say how much we love them!

These are all very different, yet they all have one feature in common: that every visit to one of these places provokes intense emotions. Some for the incredible talent of the chef, some for their unchanging classic dishes, some for the fact that they are still completely full at 10pm, some for their kindness, some for their grace (and their grease), some for their goodwill, their feelgood factor, their unquestionable desire to provide pleasure to every customer who is ready to receive it.

Here are our 8 best bistros, which range from the small 15€ menu to the places reviewed in the *New York Times*, from the 1950s to the 2000s, from typical, homely Gallic charm to the height of Parisian refinement. The *crème de la crème*, as some people say. And that cream's rather delicious.

LE COMPTOIR DU RELAIS

Odéon – €€€€ | Terrace

Yves Camdeborde was the brilliant originator of bistronomy in the 1990s, and his feats as a jury member on TV cooking shows made him even more famous. His cooking deserves its continued praise, and that is exactly what it gets every night of the week from the twenty patient hedonists who are ready to suffer through the huge line (as long as a day without wine) to sit down to a 60€ set dinner.

The produce is good, the technique is impeccable, the plates are beautiful and generous, the recipes are creative... the chef unveils just how good he is during these dinners. But don't despair! You can also enjoy the amazing Art Deco setting at lunchtime. Lunch set menus are less pricy; you can come without a reservation (although you should come early) and eat all the classics for 30 to 50€.

The mood is congenial and chatty. The dishes are always very fresh, the cooking precise and generous. Foie gras, brandade, sweetbread, spring chicken, rum baba, rice pudding... This should be enough to convey the strength of this cuisine made with passion and genuine love for authentic French food, where the chef's southwestern origins are never far away.

➡ Le Comptoir du Relais
9, carrefour de l'Odéon, 75006
Phone: 01 44 27 07 50
Mᵒ Odéon
www.hotel-paris-relais-saint-germain.com/flash/fr

Open every day

● For dinner, Monday to Friday, 60€ set menu
● Free choice for lunch and weekend dinners, 30–50€

CHEZ NÉNESSE

Filles-du-Calvaire – €€€€ | Fries on Thursdays

This place smells of the good old days. The famous Nénesse isn't here anymore, but the Leplu family, who took over this bistro, kept its good-heartedness and dated charm. You go there to taste nice, nostalgic family dishes prepared with expertise by the chef. The recipes are sometimes simplistic (which we adore), but they are executed neatly and they never fail to satisfy. Snail cassolettes, Lyonnaise pike quenelles, chicken with morels, veal head with gribiche sauce, sweetbreads, fries... the whole of French culinary tradition is firmly attached to the menu. With its typical setting of checkerboard tiles, an old oil-fired stove, a bar, and wooden tables with checkered tablecloths, this place is ideal if you want to take a non-Parisian out

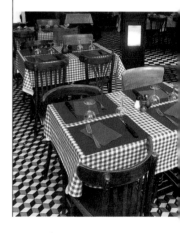

to discover typical French culture.

It is located in the heart of the Marais and is frequented by gallery owners and construction workers alike. The very reasonable pricing make it a must-go. To finish the meal properly, add a glass of Calvados to your coffee.

GRAND CŒUR

Beaubourg – €€€€ | Terrace

Mauro Colagreco is one of our favorite chefs. He is in charge of a first-class restaurant called Mirazur near the Mediterranean, in Menton. Now he is also at the head of a wonderful Parisian restaurant where he tones his ambitions down (it is not a restaurant but a brasserie, according to the name card) without toning down his talent. In the golden light of this bistro, where gigantic mirrors emerge from stone walls, in this charming *chiaroscuro* of deep blues, marble and brass, nighttime makes for the perfect setting.

On your plate, you will find the Mauro touch, of course, adapted to a style that is simple without being simplistic. The rolled-up vegetables are crunchy, light, and round; the perfectly textured lobster reclines gently in a delicate verbena broth, but explodes in your mouth with the strength of the sea; the shoulder of lamb is slowly cooked for fourteen hours before being pieced back together and seared, and takes on a sophisticated crunch next to the sweet potato; dried fruits, fine semolina, and a crème caramel served on a bed of *dulce de leche* ensnare you with their devilish unctuousness. This is a brasserie indeed, but not a chic one. To drink, there are very nice bottles at a reasonable price (which is so rare).

So, if you add to that the fact that the bill isn't too high, that you can lunch there for 30€, and that there is a huge terrace which opens onto a nice, small, paved courtyard, what's left for you to do? Run there!

➡️ **Chez Nénesse**
17, rue de Saintonge, 75003
Phone: 01 42 78 46 49
M° Filles-du-Calvaire

Closed on Saturday and Sunday

● For lunch, full menu for about 15€
● Free choice for about 40€

➡️ **Grand Cœur**
41, rue du Temple, 75004
Phone: 01 58 28 18 90
M° Rambuteau
or Hôtel-de-Ville
www.grandcoeur.paris

Closed on Monday

● Lunch set menus for 23€ and 30€
● Free choice between 40€ and 60€

× **GRAND CŒUR** ×

Grand coeur means "big heart" in French, and Mauro Colagreco definitely has that, as well as talent. Run there to discover the bistro version of this starred chef's recipes from the Mirazur in Menton.

× **LE PANTRUCHE** ×

In this bistro in South Pigalle, you will dream of becoming a regular when you take your first bite: this place offers excellent value for money.

LE BISTROT PAUL BERT

Nation – €€€€ | Small terrace – Seasonal game

A typical Parisian bistro in all its splendor! Tourists (mostly American and Japanese) usually start by marveling at the nostalgic setting with the red sofas, old posters, tiles, and the chalkboards hung up on the walls. Then, like the rest of the gourmets and regulars, they are delighted by the menu and the endless pleasures it promises.

Parisians have been eating at this institution of a restaurant on rue Paul-Bert for over a decade. The food and service are comforting and generous. Everything calls for self-indulgence and good spirits. The bistro presents French classics like no other, it is attentive to the quality of the produce, to the cooking and the seasoning. This makes for hearty, traditional yet lively dishes. Those with a big appetite can finish their meal with the star dessert of the house, the huge Paris-Brest. With over a hundred listings, the wine list looks like an encyclopedia and offers a wide range of prices.

In short, you'll seldom be disappointed by this monument of French bistronomy, both affordable and comfortable. Unless, of course, you forget to book a table...

➡️ **Le Bistrot Paul Bert**
18, rue Paul-Bert, 75011
Phone: 01 43 72 24 01
Mᵒ Charonne

Closed on Sunday and Monday

● Lunch set menu for 19€
● Dinner set menu for 38€

L'ASSIETTE

Denfert-Rochereau – €€€€ | Seasonal game

If you're not feeling well, take a trip to L'Assiette. This former neighborhood deli was transformed into a bistro by Lucienne Rousseau, the renowned Lulu, who can count among her most famous customers a certain President François Mitterrand. David Rathgeber took it over and changed the name of the restaurant but kept the setting, with its engraved windows and incredible ceilings.

In the kitchen, the talented chef, who previously worked with Alain Ducasse, serves up homely dishes in a bourgeois atmosphere. The blue shrimp tartar is stunning, the olive and pine nuts have a striking savor, the oxtail pâté has character, and the essential cassoulet is made up, on top of the traditional mogette bean from the Vendée, of duck confit, pork ribs, garlic sausage, and lamb neck. No wonder, as this particular chef is a

member of the Universal Cassoulet Academy! It's an iconic dish that represents the true *gourmandise* celebrated by this bistro. The desserts are no less good: the chocolate fondant is divine and the crème caramel is unbelievably unctuous. This is one place where the generosity isn't feigned.

LE PANTRUCHE

Pigalle – €€€€

This bistro, created by Franck Baranger and Edouard Bobin, has been fully booked ever since it opened in South Pigalle. That's because it offers a good value for money, and the rare talents of a chef who knows how to twist the habits he gained when he was working for great restaurants – Franck used to work for Eric Fréchon at the Bristol.

The cooks know how to make gravy, a sauce, a low-temperature egg, or poach poultry, and everything is combined with sensitivity and balance: chestnuts in celeriac velouté, oyster tartar on lettuce cream, sweet potato mousseline alongside scallops, salt cod siphon on a leek fondue... The Grand Marnier soufflé with salted caramel is now iconic. The staff are extremely welcoming and there is a fine wine list. The clientele consists mostly of regulars – and you'll dream of becoming one on your second mouthful.

➡ L'Assiette
181, rue du Château, 75014
Phone: 01 43 22 64 86
M° Pernety, Alésia,
Gaîté or Mouton-Duvernet
www.restaurant-lassiette.com

**Closed on Monday
and Tuesday**

● For lunch, 25€ set menu,
except on Sunday
● Free choice for about 50€

➡ Le Pantruche
3, rue Victor-Massé, 75009
Phone: 01 48 78 55 60
M° Pigalle or Saint-Georges

**Closed on Saturday
and Sunday**

● Lunch set menu for 18€
● Free choice for 34€

L'AMI JEAN
Invalides – €€€€

There really is no need to introduce this place anymore – the whole of Paris (and beyond) is in awe of it! Everyone knows that, in order to sit at a table there, you need a strong character and an all-conquering appetite, because this beast isn't easy to tame! Sure, the wooden interior and the menu have recently been lightened, but the chef Stéphane Jégo's talent hasn't. He is an expert in creating casual dishes that use the best seasonal produce in inspired recipes that nod toward the rich cuisine of southwest France, and are at once rustic, creative, and forward-looking.

In this temple of Parisian bistronomy, you still eat the same huge plates (the size of which are noted in the prices – let's not dream), the same classic game dishes (among them a whole hare *à la royale*), the same surprising earth and sea pairings, and the monumental rice pudding!

All of this can be enjoyed in a magical atmosphere, alongside tourists who have had their fill for a week, grouchy wait staff, and big eaters. If you go there to celebrate, the wine list will provide you with all you need!

➡ **L'Ami Jean**
27, rue Malar, 75007
Phone: 01 47 05 86 89
M° Invalides
or La Tour-Maubourg
www.lamijean.fr

**Closed on Sunday
and Monday**

● For lunch, 35€ and 55€
set menus
● For dinner, 78€ menu
● Free choice for about 80€

CHEZ MARCEL
Montparnasse – €€€€

This is the kind of bistro that makes Americans fall in love with Paris. In its DNA is an assessment of the appetites that's stuck somewhere in the 1960s. In 2012, Chez Marcel was taken over by Pierre Cheucle, a self-taught cook who was taken under Eric Fréchon's wing, and the chef decided not to make any changes to a bistro that had already been successful for fifty years. The setting is the same: a joyful jumble of souvenirs with wallflower paper, small posters, still lives, and grandma's lampshades.

In the kitchen, Pierre lets the chef who had already been there for 25 years continue to do his magic and keep cooking – with only small alterations – the menu that was created in 1961 on a typewriter, and which is now in the restaurant's archives. Herring, Burgundy escargots, quenelles, tripe, and coq au vin all form a

delicious cuisine that makes a real impact. Pierre has added a few specialties such as a pork carpaccio with capers and condiments, a cuttlefish tagliatelle (a must-have that is both crunchy, tender, and spicy), and a praline tart so sweet almost a sin – without forgetting the game served during the season.

It doesn't take any more than that to get a bunch of cheerful diners to go to Chez Marcel and chat across tables, full of warm-hearted *bel esprit*, incredibly happy to be there. And believe us, you will be too.

➡️ **Chez Marcel**
7, rue Stanislas, 75006
Phone: 01 45 48 29 94
Mᵒ Vavin
or Notre-Dame-des-Champs

Closed on Saturday and Sunday

● Lunch set menu for 19€
● Free choice, between 40 and 50€ for lunch; 60 and 70€ for dinner

× **CHEZ MARCEL** ×

In this provincial bistro, a strong repertoire
makes a crowd of joyful diners incredibly happy.

David Abiker's

VIEW ON BISTROS
—◆—

Journalist

In *Being and Nothingness,* Sartre describes the dance of the Parisian waiter perfectly. "He has lively and urgent gestures that are a bit too precise, a bit too quick, he approaches customers with a step that is too lively, he leans towards them with slightly too much intent, his voice, his eyes express an interest too full of concern for the customer's order, and here he comes again, trying to imitate the walk of a robot, rigorous and unbending, all the while carrying his tray with the assurance of a tightrope walker (...). He plays, he has fun. What is he playing at? You don't need to observe him for long to realize that he is playing at being a waiter."

I am not sure that Sartre liked this little game, but I do, and I do all the more now that it has become so rare. Yves Montand portrayed it perfectly in *Garçon!* by Claude Sautet, a filmmaker who loved shooting scenes in bistros. Sartre, Montand, and Sautet are all gone, but there are still a few brasseries in Paris where good and lively wait staff play at being *garçons*, and that's rather neat.

Among them there is Le Stella, close to my house. Seafood, sole meunière, steak with pepper sauce, pâté, egg mayo: nothing new on the plate, or in the world, but that is exactly what I love about the Stella. It is a sublime uproar against the foodie culture, whose disciples linger eagerly on TripAdvisor. No, you go to the Stella as one who respects institutions and passing time and friendships that last, not wanting to celebrate New Year's eve. Everything is a certainty there. The red paint on the walls, the everlasting font on the menu, the opening hours, and the dessert. As far as I'm concerned, the dessert is always the same: vacherin cake with blackberries, almonds, and a meringue. As for the wait staff, all of them remind me of a distant cousin who lives far from Paris, and they all have the elegance to act according to the Sartre playbook. And they do it well, too.

Le Stella
133, avenue Victor-Hugo, 75016
Phone: 01 56 90 56 00
M° Victor-Hugo

Garçon ! — Claude Sautet (1983)

THE BISTRONOMY HEROES

Let's be clear: Paris owes them everything. The new culinary landscape of Paris is thanks to them. They have revolutionized Parisian restaurants and led the way for the renewal of bistros, which is happening on every street corner, right now.

If life on a plate is now so fertile, exuberant, and full of surprises and flavors, we owe it to these chefs: Constant, Camdeborde, Breton, Jégo, Paquin... These generous men who love bistro life, and life in general, were the first ones to leave the grandest, Michelin-starred tables in Paris (such as Crillon, Ritz, Bristol) to open up small places with no tablecloths but lots of talent. They combined the know-how of high gastronomy with the simple desire to welcome people. They revived the almost forgotten verb: *restaurer*, to restore.

These are the true simplifiers, the pioneers who dared to introduce bistro dishes revitalized with technique, creativity, and precision, and worthy of the best gourmet restaurants. Paris welcomed them with open arms, and Parisians with open stomachs.

This is our way of paying homage to the heroes of bistronomy, without whom none of this food revolution would have happened, and who have been treating us to great meals since the early 1990s.

L'ÉPI DUPIN

Rue de Rennes – €€€€ | Large tables

François Pasteau has been managing this lovely place on the chic Left Bank for ten years. The décor is charming but has attitude, with rustic stone and robust wooden timbers that run up to the ceiling, exposed beams, black and wooden furniture, industrial lamps, and good wine bottles perched up high. This modern setting is not cold in the least: service is warm and welcoming, and you eat in a friendly atmosphere. You'd have to be pretty grouchy to not enjoy the food here, which honors home cooking: delicious and sometimes full of surprises.

Since the beginning, this secret address has navigated the trends without making waves, but with an amazing sense of direction. Dishes change with each season, and are always attentive to produce (all local – even the bread is homemade). The menu celebrates tradition, but isn't afraid to play with recipes (veal and whelk), flavors (citrus vinaigrette), and a few tastes of foreign lands. It is refined, creative, and incredibly well made. And the cherry on the cake is that it's not even that expensive. That's quite a feat in this neighborhood! You might even use it as an opportunity to do some shopping at the Bon Marché right around the corner, like the beautiful regulars from Saint-Germain-des-Prés.

➡ **L'Épi Dupin**
11, rue Dupin, 75006
Phone: 01 42 22 64 56
M° Rennes
www.epidupin.com

Closed on Saturday and Sunday

● Lunch set menu for 28€
● For dinner, 39€ regular menu or gourmet menu for 52€

L'ENTREDGEU

Champerret – €€€€ | Seasonal game

Breaking with the current trend of naming your restaurant Encore, Beaucoup, Manger, or Table, this bistro's name is a word play based on the owner's last name, Tredgeu, however impossible to pronounce that is! Bucking the trends once more, they chose a location in an unexpected, isolated neighborhood at Porte de Champerret. Even there, between the regulars that live nearby, the passersby, and the gourmets who pass each other the address under the table, the tables are always full! The décor is unoriginal and not particularly worth the trip: red benches, counter, woodwork, and checkerboard tiles.

➡ **L'Entredgeu**
83, rue Laugier, 75017
Phone: 01 40 54 97 24
M° Porte-de-Champerret

Closed on Sunday and Monday

● Lunch set menu for 26€
● Dinner menu 36€

To fully understand this place's popularity, you have to look at the food. The chef has been preparing seasonal dishes with Basque influences since forever (look out for the game in Autumn), along with bistronomy classics cooked and served perfectly: grilled pigs' ears, duck and foie gras tart, roasted scallops, Béarnais black boudin, all roll easily off the chalkboard. The dishes are brought to you by a warm (sometimes a little over-excited) team of wait staff, and reveal precise cooking that is skillful at mixing and matching flavors. In this little room, excited by the boldness of the dishes and the wine list (short, smart, and affordable), you'll congratulate yourself for coming!

LA RÉGALADE

Alésia – €€€€ | Seasonal game

What a challenge: to take over Yves Camdeborde's restaurant and fill the shoes of this giant of bistro cooking, to continue to get people to come to the 14th arrondissement, and to open two other restaurants simultaneously! Bruno Doucet was up to the task, and succeeded brilliantly. To taste his bourgeois cuisine, which is exciting and straightforward, we'd gladly travel to Porte d'Orléans every day.

Thankfully for people who live in the city center, you won't have to, since the two new locations are in the 1st and 9th arrondissements. You'll find the same seasonal menu in all three locations, which is a love letter to the cooking and traditions of southwest France. The names of the dishes sound basic, but the cooking is surprisingly delicate, and they are made with incredible technique. You'll tuck in eagerly with your fork, experiencing true joy. The perfect menu? The *terrine de campagne* (left as an offering on the table by the waiter), the hare civet, when available, (it's a deadly sin), and the rice pudding (which is even better than the one your grandma used to make). With good wine, and served with *bonhomie*: that's a delicious meal!

➡ **La Régalade**
49, avenue Jean-Moulin, 75014
Phone: 01 45 45 68 58
M° Alésia or Porte-d'Orléans

Closed for lunch on Monday, all day Saturday and Sunday

● For lunch and dinner, 37€ menu
● Free choice around 60€

× **LA RÉGALADE** ×

Bourgeois cuisine, straightforward but exciting: a love letter to the traditions and
cooking of southwest France. A restaurant that spoils its guests!

LE BEURRE NOISETTE

Convention – €€€€ | Large tables – Private room available

If you're in the neighborhood (and even if you aren't), don't miss out on the implacable charm of Beurre Noisette. Thierry Blanqui's tables are set away from the hurly burly of the street, and suggest nothing extravagant when you take a first look: nice white tablecloths for a good-mannered little bistro. But the food is impressive and always right on point. High bistronomy!

On the small chalkboard, a few appetizers, entrées, and desserts are offered, made from the day's ideas and produce. One the plate are nice lessons in traditional cooking, sincere and inspired. Here's a sneek peak to get you salivating: last time we were there, we had black boudin ravioli with spicy broth and a haddock brandade with green cabbage. Like most regulars (and there are a lot of them), we chose the ambergris-perfumed rum baba for dessert. It is iconic, with its vanilla-honey cream and the bottle of Saint-James that comes with it. The wine list displays the same serene fortitude. And the check isn't even that big – go figure!

➡ **Le Beurre Noisette**
68, rue Vasco-de-Gama, 75015
Phone: 01 48 56 82 49
Mᵒ Balard or Porte-de-Versailles

Closed on Sunday and Monday

● For lunch, menu between 23€ and 31€
● For dinner, 35€ to 55€ menus

CHEZ MICHEL

Boulevard de Magenta – €€€€

Along the little rue de Belzunce, Thierry Breton has built an empire. He manages three restaurants there, all lively and offering varied pleasures. At number 10, Chez Marcel, the traditional watering hole is revamped with Armorican (Brittany) vibes. The décor all in woodwork, makes the place look like a coastal inn, and looks as boring as a government building, but the cooking has character!

This is not surprising, given that Thierry Breton is a pioneer of great Parisian bistronomy. Classics on the chalkboard are pimped with a Breton twist. Here, produce is king, and like all kings, it is very well dressed and presented. The house specialty is the Breton pot-au-feu (a *kig ha farz* in the local language): it is a savory and filling dish, able to put any sailor fresh from Cape Horn back on his feet! We kept the best for last: the huge Paris-Brest, made to order with crunchy caramelized nuts, is enough

➡ **Chez Michel**
10, rue de Belzunce, 75010
Phone: 01 44 53 06 20
Mᵒ Gare-du-Nord

Closed on Saturday and Sunday

● For lunch, menu between 29€ and 35€
● For dinner, 35€ menus
● Picnic baskets in the summer, 54€ for two to three people

in itself to justify going there. We love the service, although it can be a bit rough around the edges, and we salute the good prices, although the extras are sometimes killjoys.

CHEZ PHILOU

Canal Saint-Martin – €€©© | Terrace – Game – Nice wines

The foodies who are not easily fooled by the short-lived popularity of the canal Saint-Martin eateries have found refuge at Chez Philou. In the shade by the gardens of the Saint-Louis hospital, Philippe Damas (he's Philou) is a former Crillon and Square Trousseau chef (another baby-Constant) who has been celebrating bistronomy in this clean little bistro for a few years now. In this setting of dark wood and red banquettes, huge chalkboards announce the menu of classics made with drum-beating talent.

A few essentials from bistro gastronomy are to be found here, like frogs' legs, scallops, beef cheek, or free-range chicken fricassee. Don't miss the made-to-order Paris-Brest: it's sinfully good. During the right season, customers are lured here by the game (partridge tart, Scottish grouse, roasted pheasant...)

Lunching at Chez Philou is like being with friends: the friendly and joyful atmosphere runs from table to table, and it's contagious. The mood is made all the warmer by the beautiful wine selection from local producers, offered by the proprietor who now works on the other side of the kitchen. Here again, the chef Shin Maeda is Japanese, and prepares the plates with dexterity. Thankfully, he has switched from soy sauce to butter. We won't argue with that.

➡ **Chez Philou**
12, avenue Richerand, 75010
Phone: 01 42 38 00 13
M° Goncourt
www.restophilou.com

**Closed on Sunday
and Monday**

● Menus at 24€, 32€
and 38€

LE REPAIRE DE CARTOUCHE
Bastille – €€€€
Out-of-this-world *pâté en croûte* – Seasonal game

Cartouche was the king of thieves, so his den has to be roguish. If you enjoy honest places and food with character, you've come to the right place (and there are even two of them!). Rodolphe Paquin is a remarkable and charismatic chef who has been working here for fifteen years. The dishes he puts together are robust and frank, full of precision, and delicious. Meat and game eaters, pay attention: during the game season, the hare *à la royale* is a must-eat, just like the terrine and the *pâté en croûte*, the owner's two guilty pleasures.

Everything is set to the rhythm of changing seasons, and you'll enjoy every second of your meal, whether you choose to end it with a cheese platter or one of the excellent desserts on offer. The wine list is organic and natural, well composed, and won't hike up the check up too much. The décor used to be full of woodwork with a musketeer vibe, but it was recently remodeled – it had to be done. With the service, you've a 50-50 chance to get either the best waiter in Paris, or the worst. The evening will be memorable either way!

➡ **Le Repaire de Cartouche**
8, boulevard des Filles-du-Calvaire, 75011
Phone: 01 47 00 25 86
Mᵒ Saint-Sébastien-Froissart

Closed on Sunday and Monday

● Lunch set menus between 20€ and 30€
● Dinner between 50€ and 60€

× **LE REPAIRE DE CARTOUCHE** ×

In this roguish bistro — Cartouche was the king of thieves — the atmosphere is honest, and the food has character. The perfect den for game-lovers!

MOVIE-LOVERS' BISTROS

Did you ever notice how much people eat in the movies? And drink too, of course. In the 1970s, actors even smoked a lot on screen. Remember Claude Sautet's films? There isn't a single one that doesn't contain a scene in which people eat. In over-populated bistros with clouds of smoke and invigorating daily specials, in chic brasseries where the wait staff wear long black aprons, groups of friends, romantic diners, Cesar and Rosalie... Sautet filmed life. And life also went on at the bistro.

And the 1950s? *Monsieur Gangster* and black-and-white films. Lino Ventura ordered veal *paupiettes*, Jean Gabin had a soft spot for *blanquette*, and *The Trip Across Paris* carried a pig in its luggage. Bank raids were planned at the bar, and Paul Meurisse, wearing an eyeglass, intoxicated young girls with his deep voice. The bistro owner was a whole other character. He presented the week's menu, shouted at the wait staff, and had a fight with his wife before showing you to the phone booth. So many love stories were born sitting at one of those tables, so many negotiations took place there, so many break-ups, and so many proposals.

But a bistro is also a theater, one where the French language can make the most unique moments of life the most mundane, from ordering food from a menu to the most perfect state of drunkenness. A theater where humanity plays itself for a plate of lentils, where secrets are shared like glasses of moonshine.

Un singe en hiver – Henri Verneuil (1962)

We remember the words that Michel Audiard put in Gabin's mouth in the film *A Monkey in Winter*, in 1962:

"Oh, you mix all of it up! My Spanish, as you say, with old Bardas, the grand dukes, and the stuff you drink when you're not thirsty!

- The grand dukes?

- Yes, sir! The princes of drunkenness, the lords, the people you used to drink with, but who always drank from a different glass. Tell yourself that: they let you and your clients deal with your shit, the lords, they're 100,000 glasses ahead of you. They... they're on first-name terms with angels!"

That says it all.

PARISIAN HISTORY

This is the beating heart of Paris. These restaurants have been spreading the aroma of potatoes and herrings *à l'huile*, boudin with mashed potatoes, and roasted chicken around the city for decades. They are in Parisians' lives just like a première at the Garnier opera house, or a strike from Bastille to Nation. Without them, Paris simply wouldn't be Paris.

We have lunch there in surroundings like a stage set, we feel it can't change, set as if in Madeira wine jelly. We dine among opera-house décor with rumors from centuries gone by trickling down the walls. We raise our glasses to the memory of our glorious ancestors, to at-table service on a pedestal, and flambéed crèpes, we drink to 15-course menus and weekly specials. But we can't smoke there anymore.

Their names will definitely ring a bell: Allard, Chez Savy, Le Voltaire, Chez Georges, Joséphine, Pharamond... Whether they began life in the 1950s or in the nineteenth century, in the era of horse-drawn carriages and top hats, they all evoke something of the Parisian spirit.

This is, no doubt, why so many tourists go there, sure to find a piece of history to taste in between sips of Bordeaux. It's also why these places are so charming, and why Parisians should rush there to make them their own again. Here are our favorites.

LE VOLTAIRE

Musée d'Orsay – €€€€ | Terrace

Le Voltaire is an icon of bourgeois cooking: you have to go there at least once. Sure, this time-travelling meal is not within everybody's budget, but to ply your fork at such a historic address is certainly worth the few extra euros! Ministers, actresses, and other rich people from both sides of the Atlantic are often seen sitting on the beautiful terrace, facing the booksellers on the bank of the Seine, or inside the tree-filled space with an old-fashioned and cozy charm.

The menu shows the merits of the classic repertoire, and keeps one small anomaly going: the eggs mayonnaise resist the current trend and are still sold 90 cents... Despite the very low price – and this is where the pride of the house is exemplified – it is delicious, and comes with a generous portion of crunchy vegetables. This ironic and light appetizer is a perfect introduction to the rest. Meats and fish follow with their remarkable sauces (béarnaise, pepper, mustard...), and with plenty of deliciously crisp fries. The dishes are generous and placed on the table by a courteous and cheerful wait staff in white sleeves, who are just as out of time and pleasant as the décor. Now, since you're here, you may as well do things right and open up a good bottle at an insolent price. You only live once.

➡ Le Voltaire
27, quai Voltaire, 75007
Phone: 01 42 61 17 49
M° Solférino or Palais-Royal-Musée du Louvre

Closed on Sunday and Monday

● Free choice for about 80€

L'ÉPI D'OR

Louvre-Les Halles – €€€€

You'll travel through time when you walk through the doors of this bistro, located close to the Halles. These kitchens have been open since 1880 and they've seen quite a lot of customers go by, ranging from the workers of the neighborhood (dubbed the Paris Stomach) to the ficklest night owls. Nothing seems to have changed over time, from the Belle Epoque décor to the robust and traditional cooking. Even the regulars look like they have been stuck to their tables for years.

In this surreal atmosphere, you can eat dishes that seem to have escaped from another century, cooked with respect for tradition: potatoes and herrings à l'huile, a wonderful leg of lamb, generous calves' liver

meunière, gratin dauphinois, crème caramel, and clafoutis made from seasonal fruits. It isn't cheap (around 40€ per person), but it is good, and you'll leave feeling completely full. The portions are generous – small appetites will suffer, and so will sensitive types, because the service, cocky yet friendly, can get slightly hammy.

LE SQUARE TROUSSEAU

Bastille – €€€€
Terrace – Full-time service – Private room available

You must stop by here, if only to take a picture and immortalize this splendid décor straight out of the Roaring Twenties (the place opened in 1907, to be exact)! Underneath yellowing ceilings, engraved mirrors, ceiling lights and stucco, ancient molding, a precious counter, cream-colored seats, and wait staff dressed in their best all form a charming and refined picture. Just like in the 1930s, this place attracts a distinguished, well-dressed clientele in the evenings, and a more touristy crowd for lunch.

On the plate, you will taste the Costes dynasty. The produce is skillfully chosen: at Square Trousseau, only the best is cooked, and only for the best! The menu is well conceived (and heavily priced, some might say) and offers a wide range of food to please both fathers and daughters. For him, a veal escalope with cream and mushrooms; for her, the swordfish with arugula and lemon olive oil. The prices (slightly over the edge) and some irregularities in the food may make you want to eat elsewhere. But trust us: once you've settled on the heated terrace, with a sweeping view of the park that gave its name to the bistro, you'll forget all that.

➤ **L'Épi d'Or**
25, rue Jean-Jacques-Rousseau, 75001
Phone: 01 42 36 38 12
M° Louvre-Rivoli
or Les Halles
www.faget-benard.com/jojo/epidor

Closed for lunch on Saturday, and on Sunday

● Lunch set menus at 17€ and 23€
● Free choice for about 40€

➤ **Le Square Trousseau**
1, rue Antoine-Vollon, 75012
Phone: 01 43 43 06 00
M° Ledru-Rollin
www.squaretrousseau.com

Open every day

● Free choice for about 40€ to 50€

× **LE SQUARE TROUSSEAU** ×
Décor straight out of the Roaring Twenties, a well-conceived menu for all tastes,
and a heated terrace! Let the charm do its work...

PHARAMOND
Les Halles – €€€€ | Terrace – Private rooms available

Paris is full of places that make you travel through time, where you can still detect the aromas of past decades. This place was frequented by the Lost Generation in the 1920s (Fitzgerald and Hemingway both tried French gastronomy here) and by politicians in the 1970s and 80s (François Mitterrand was a regular). The Pharamond has barely changed since then. The spirit of ancient times is still here, behind the timbering, in the Parisian décor with its woodwork, mirrors, molten glass, and earthenware from the Universal Exhibition in 1900; and in the provincial cooking.

The food smells of all-time Normandy: *andouillette* in generous portions, tripe from maison Ruault (in Vire) served in fondue pots, soft and gelatinous just the way we like it (people say that Jacques Chirac used to get it delivered to the Paris City-Hall); veal ribs from the Auge valley; well-kept cheeses with cider, just as if you were under the trees in the orchard at Pont-Audemer... It's generous and sincere food that goes straight to the point, and doesn't make a fuss. To top it all, there's a lesser-known last floor, where several living rooms are ornate with a 1900 boudoir style. You can, of course, secrete yourself there behind closed doors between courses... This place is full of surprises, including the rather reasonable prices.

➡ **Pharamond**
24, rue de la Grande-Truanderie, 75001
Phone: 01 40 28 45 18
Mᵒ Étienne-Marcel
www.pharamond.fr

Open every day

● Lunch set menu at 15.50€
● Menus from 29.90 to 39.90€
● Free choice for about 35-45€

LA FONTAINE DE MARS
Champ de Mars – €€€€
Terrace – Large tables – Private room available

In a small street in the 7ᵗʰ arrondissement, just steps away from the Eiffel Tower, this gourmet bistro is one of the oldest in Paris, and seems out of time. It is chic and classic, with a superb counter, moleskin seats, Vichy checkered fabric, and ancient flooring. This typical Parisian décor pleases Americans (including Obama), and serves traditional food, as precise as it is *gourmet*.

Here, you don't mess with tradition: the wait staff are dressed to the nines, the daily specials follow a weekly order (on Monday, the butcher's special; on Tuesday, salted pork, etc.), made to the same recipes

with which they've always treated their regulars. If the regulars could advise you, they would probably mention the eggs mayonnaise with small crudités, the Basque boudin, or the roasted leg of lamb on Thursdays. They would also mention the desserts, especially the chocolate mousse or floating islands. These classics may sound boring, but they are actually amazing, and so good you may even forget how expensive they are! Come here in winter to enjoy the game and the mushrooms, and in summer to enjoy the terrace that faces the fountain of the god Mars. In Paris, the 7th is a village.

CHEZ DENISE
LA TOUR DE MONTLHÉRY

Les Halles — €€€€

It is three in the morning, and, behind the timbering, Denise's priceless bistro lights up the night in Les Halles like a lighthouse. All the gregarious people in Paris meet there to eat beef, tripe, or veal kidney, served in gigantic portions! They come for the cooking (which is not always precise) as much as for the atmosphere in this historic, friendly, and very French bistro.

Underneath Moretti lithographs, the tables are close together and will be shared without fuss. Good wine flows abundantly (note the excellent Côte-de-Brouilly) and it is sold *à la ficelle* (which means you only pay for what you drink). The atmosphere is exhilarating, as are the prices! We advise you to go there with a group of friends, to gather strength during an all-nighter, but definitely not with your girlfriend or boyfriend, unless you want to break up. If this is the case, this may actually be a safe bet. He or she will still find you less mean than the wait staff, will be able to drown his or her sorrow in a magnificent rum baba, and go home with one of the numerous tourists who come here to get drunk.

➡ La Fontaine de Mars
129, rue Saint-Dominique, 75007
Phone: 01 47 05 46 44
M° École-Militaire
or La Tour-Maubourg
www.fontainedemars.com
Two other addresses:
Le Petit Cler, 29, rue Cler, 75007 and Café de l'Alma, 5, avenue Rapp, 75007

Open every day

● Daily special at 22€
● Free choice for about 35-70€

➡ Chez Denise
– La Tour de Montlhéry
5, rue des Prouvaires, 75001
Phone: 01 42 36 21 82
M° Les Halles

Closed Saturday and Sunday
Open until 5am

● Free choice for about 50-70€

ALLARD

Saint-Germain-des-Prés – €€€€

This is the typical Saint-Germain bistro – the one that Minnesotans dream of! This ancient house in the Latin Quarter, with its varnished wood out front, has seen the hottest celebrities in the city pass through since 1931. All this glory may seem outdated, but that's without taking into account the interest Alain Ducasse himself took in this place with its post-war Parisian décor. He manages this place with white tablecloths, an impressive counter, ancient wallpaper, red seats, and a sparkling kitchen, and installed chef Laëtitia Rouabah there to head the kitchen. She knows how to cook iconic traditional dishes while still updating them, lightly and with a modern touch.

➡ **Allard**

1, rue de l'Éperon, 75006
Phone: 01 43 26 48 23
M° Saint-Michel

Open every day

● Lunch set menu at 34€
● Free choice for about 80€

You enter through the kitchen, and we recommend you head toward the right (it's the nicest room, in our opinion). You'll eat the best frisée salad with lardons in the city, hot escargots from Burgundy, or a roasted chicken whose meat, jus, and accompanying fries are sinfully good. It's to be expected that a show like this, on your plate and in the surroundings, comes at a price. But since the quality is there, and the service is effective and attentive, despite the constant flow of customers (consider booking), we'll forget to complain.

JOSÉPHINE CHEZ DUMONET

Montparnasse – €€€€ | Terrace

I want to talk to you about a time you can't have known if you're less than 20 years old. About traditional cooking, about an out-of-time bistro with tableware art straight from another era. When they took over this place more than twenty years ago, Mr. Dumonet (the chef) and his wife (who illuminates the room with her smile), managed to keep its gourmet spirit alive, to the great joy of American tourists, out-of-towners, regulars, and gourmands everywhere!

They all enjoy the food in the chic and traditional décor, with tablecloths as bright as the silverware. The wait staff run around in aprons with unexpected coolness to distribute the grand house classics. Sweetbread for table 2 (surely one of the best in Paris), a lamb leg for 5 (book it, to make sure you can taste it), and two Grand Marnier soufflés for table 10! Here, the produce doesn't lie. It's well bred, well chosen, and cooked with generosity, talent, and know-how. If you go there for lunch, be careful, it's a trap! At the Dumonets', you'll always have trouble leaving. And don't count on the wine list (classic, expensive, but impeccable), or the incredible liquor selection to help you out!

➡ **Joséphine**
– Chez Dumonet
117, rue du Cherche-Midi, 75006
Phone: 01 45 48 52 40
M° Duroc or Saint-Placide

Closed on Saturday and Sunday

● Free choice for about 70€

LESCURE

Concorde – €€€€ | Terrace

A little *auberge* from another time. Steps away from Concorde, close to the Jeu de Paume, time stopped here at the beginning of the twentieth century. The rustic décor is the same as when the place opened in 1919 (a counter with saucissons and braided onions, a straw hat collection, heavy wood tables), and the recipes were all passed on from generation to generation in the owner's family, which was originally from Corrèze. Try the chicken pâté, Burgundy escargots, poached haddock, boeuf bourguignon, Henri IV stuffed braised chicken, crème caramel, red fruit vacherin... All of this comes at reasonable prices (menu for 25€, 15€ for an entrée), served nicely and in a welcoming atmosphere, in the old-time way.

➡ **Lescure**
7, rue de Mondovi, 75001
Phone: 01 42 60 18 91
M° Concorde
www.lescure1919.fr

Closed on Saturday and Sunday

● For lunch and dinner, 25€ menu
● Free choice for about 30€

In this rustic atmosphere, a few astonished tourists, attracted by the folklore, and a few regulars, share the space, huddled up next to each other. The tourists will no doubt share this Parisian experience with their friends, but the Parisian regulars will want to keep this place a secret. And we get this: the terrace, with its yellow sunshades, is a gem. It offers little space, though, so sssssh, keep this one to yourselves!

× **ALLARD** ×
In this typical Saint-Germain bistro with ancient wallpaper, the food is iconic.
You will eat the best frisée salad with lardons in Paris here...

× **FLAUBERT** ×

Food from the Lyon region is served in this former grocery in a chic and traditional atmosphere.
Try the chef's very best offering: kidney and *pâté en croûte*.

CHEZ GEORGES
Bourse – €€€€

Don't confuse this iconic Parisian bistro with the one on the rue des Canettes, a wine cellar that also deserves your attention (especially if you're a student and don't mind a few red wine stains). In this bistro on rue du Mail, the ambiance is less festive, but just as lovely. Since it opened in 1964, and despite changing owners several times, this place kept its spirit and its charm. The décor is retro, chic, and in the Parisian Haussmann style. Book ahead to get a spot on the red banquettes, because this place is packed with gourmets and knowledgeable tourists. Only if you book will you get to enjoy a moment out of time, away from the crowd and culinary trends.

On the menu, you will find every cliché in the book, all more delicious than the next: potatoes and herrings *à l'huile*, escargots by the dozen, eggs mayonnaise, Henri IV kidneys, English-style calves' liver... If you're coming here for the first time, you should try this bourgeois house specialty: the mail steak, a porterhouse steak with fries and a creamy mustard sauce. This is iconic, as gourmet as it is well cooked! The rest is just as good: the cooking at Chez Georges knows how to please, and is always precise. The wine, from Bordeaux to Burgundy, can be served *à la ficelle*, and the wait staff are efficient and nicely playful. The prices, though, are less nice.

⇒ Chez Georges
1, rue du Mail, 75002
Phone: 01 42 60 07 11
M° Bourse or Sentier

Closed on Saturday and Sunday

● Lunch special for 19.50€
● Free choice for about 60€

LE BISTROT D'À CÔTÉ FLAUBERT
Ternes – €€€€ | Terrace – *Pâté en croûte*

A few feet away from his Michelin-starred restaurant, chef Michel Rostang opened this traditional and generous bistro annexe. The décor is grandiloquent: a warm mixture of marble and woodwork plays host to a playful and surprising collection of coffee grinders, old Michelin guides, and Provençal carafes with funny faces. We would come here just to sit, look around, and take in the chic and slightly folkloric atmosphere of this former grocer. Don't be distracted, though, because the show also goes on in the food!

Chef Nicolas Beaumann, who also works in the restaurant next door, wonderfully heads this kitchen that stays true to its love of dishes from the Lyon region. He cooks perfect classics (guinea fowl with cabbage, saddle of rabbit, stir-fried calamari and mussels...) with good produce and noteworthy dexterity. This eternally excellent sauce chef makes honest dishes that will touch your heart. You will eat the best *pâté en croûte* in Paris here (made from Challans duck and foie gras), and those who do not count calories will kneel before the kidney, served whole with macaroni gratin. The service is full of care, just like at Mom's. Do not miss this beautiful place.

➡ **Le Bistrot d'à côté**
– Flaubert
10, rue Gustave-Flaubert, 75017
Phone: 01 42 67 05 81
M° Ternes
www.bistrotflaubert.com

Closed for lunch on Saturday, and all day Sunday and Monday

● Lunch menus between 24€ and 29€
● Dinner menu at 36€
● Free choice for about 50€

Nicolas d'Estienne d'Orves
VIEW ON BISTROS
— ◆ —
Writer

Now, let's define the bistro. It's not a simple task, to be honest. When you say *brasserie*, you can picture mosaics from the Belle Époque, a ballet of wait staff, and mugs brimming with beer. When you hear *gastro*, the ballet is suddenly choreographed, the plates plain, and the noise toned down. A *café?* You can just smell the freshly ground coffee. But what about the bistro? There is a familiar picture of a tiny room with a busy waitress, a chef yelling in the kitchen, a chalkboard menu, neighbors that take up all the space, and a check that can go as high as the roof as quickly as it can in a three-star restaurant. But truth be told, it's the customers that make a bistro, that define and baptize it. Did the owner dream of being a restaurateur? Here he is, the bistro-owner for the gourmet customers that invade his protected space. "Here, I found a little bistro!" Already, the word makes you dream, makes you hungry. "Did you, where?" The address is passed on implicitly from one friend to the next, and hunger does the rest.

What you remember from a bistro is not a whole menu, but an entrée and a wine. You segment and focus: the kidneys at Bistro d'Henri, the horse heart at Taxi jaune, the snout salad at Ribouldingue (now closed), the andouillette at Paul Bert, the pork carpaccio at Chez Marcel... The bistro is to the restaurant what a short story is to a novel: you don't work on the length, but on the art of the outcome. You don't doll up the sentence; you aim for the effect. And when the effect has panache, brio, liveliness, and is gourmet... most of all, when it has style, you come back. *Da capo!*

D'CHEZ EUX

Champ de Mars – €€€€ | Terrace

If a bistro museum ever opened, it would look like this. Everything is there: white-and-red checkered tablecloths, saucissons hung over the bar, napkins to be tied around your neck, moleskin banquettes, varnished wooden furniture, hors d'oeuvres, and dessert buffets... Even the wait staff in aprons, professional and crabby just as they should be. Behind this stereotypical image, the cooking is gourmet, well executed and respectful of tradition – more bourgeois than it seems. You'll cross paths with a lot of celebrities here, especially politicians, who come here to eat in authentic French tradition.

The menu dismisses trends and new year's resolutions. Specialties from the Southwest and Paris mix, but the true specialty here is, without a doubt, the roasted chicken. And what a chicken it is: a rare breed from Rennes cooked with morels and cream. Of course, you can accompany this with wonderful wine: there are good bottles (mostly Bordeaux and Burgundy), but pricy. And while we are on the subject: be careful, here, if you order *à la carte*, the bill can get high.

➡ **D'chez eux**
2, avenue de Lowendal,
75007
Phone: 01 47 05 52 55
M° Saint-François-Xavier
or École-Militaire
www.chezeux.com

Open every day

● Lunch menus for 29€,
34€ and 44€ on weekends
● Free choice for about 80€

LE PETIT RÉTRO

Victor Hugo – €€€€

When you open the door of Le Petit Rétro, you put on your opera hat, adjust your monocle and take the plunge into the Art Nouveau atmosphere, complete with floral earthenware, Victoria coffee makers (branded in 1904), a timeless bar, and a display of regulars' serviettes. The Roaring Twenties have found a refuge here, with hats on racks, naughty 1920s pictures in the restrooms, varnished wooden chairs and tables under opalescent lights, and a celadon sofa.

On the menu, the classics of bistro cuisine are only slightly modernized: grated carrots with lemon and coriander, eggs mayonnaise with truffle, veal kidneys with violet mustard and Bordier butter tagliatelle, roasted salmon with basil and vegetable vermicelli, verbena-poached pears... A nice and subtle way to

rediscover these dishes. The simplicity here is well thought-out. Add a selection of a dozen wines by the glass and energetic service (it was taken over in 2013 by a former star of the small screen), and you get a bistro just as we like it: chic, but not uptight.

CHEZ SAVY

Avenue Montaigne – €€€€ | Small terrace

The entrance doesn't impress much, especially next to the stunning shops of the avenue Montaigne. But all you need to do is walk through the door to be charmed by this small bistro with a brasserie feel. The décor hasn't changed since the 1930s. In a long Art Deco room with waves of mosaic on the floor, red booths welcome a crowd of regular customers. Listen closely, because a lot of great "voices" of French radio hang out here!

If all these celebrities come eat at Savy (the restaurant was named after the previous owner), it's for the historic and truly heartwarming atmosphere, as well as for the traditional cooking. The chef is passionate: he loves good produce, and good produce loves him! On the menu, you will find classics, as well as the meat dishes that made the reputation of this place: Aubrac beef ribs, Lozère lamb shoulder, beautiful variety meats (the kidney is served whole and the *andouillette* AAAAA are must-eats)... The plates are brought to you by cocky wait staff in traditional garb. The small wine list isn't revolutionary, but it's enough to make Savy a joyful place, outside time and trends.

➡ **Le Petit Rétro**
5, rue Mesnil, 75016
Phone: 01 44 05 06 05
M° Victor-Hugo
petitretro.fr

Closed on Sunday

● Menus between 25€ and 35€
● Free choice for about 50€

➡ **Chez Savy**
23, rue Bayard, 75008
Phone: 01 47 23 46 98
M° Franklin-D.-Roosevelt
www.chezsavy.com

Closed on Saturday and Sunday

● Free choice for about 50€

LOCAL CUISINE

We can be slightly obsessive sometimes. Obsessive about *quenelles* one day, about *choucroute* the next. Sometimes, it's a whole culinary tradition that our stomachs desire, to travel intensely and profoundly through the medium of food.

These bistros, which specialize in local and traditional cuisine, are made for connoisseurs; for those that are not enticed by trendy food or TV recommendations; for the gourmets, the real ones; for people who are not scared of diet-unfriendly food; for those who know their classics, and don't discover food only on Twitter or Masterchef.

Be warned, though: these traditional bistros are reserved for true hedonists who love the simple pleasures of life. Because it's life and nothing but life that you will experience in these places, which know where food comes from. If you are ready to try *tablier de sapeur* from Lyon, cassoulet from Languedoc, and typical French *poule au pot*, here are our favorite exotic locations.

LA POULE AU POT

Les Halles – €€€€ | Small terrace

This place is almost too good to be true: a 1930s bistro in the middle of Les Halles, open all night. The promise of traditional cuisine with historical dish names and grandma's recipes. It smells like a tourist trap, yet the tourists that come here are seldom disappointed. Nor are the night owls with fine appetites who accompany them (including a lot of celebrities), who can't hide their delight.

In an old-fashioned and joyous atmosphere, this crowd eats the classics, which are no less savory for being classics, and drinks good wines, or cheap ones. The *poule au pot* is the star dish; it was Henri IV's favorite, and it lives up to its reputation. Served in a white tureen, the cooking is perfect, the broth nicely perfumed, and the vegetables melt in your mouth. But that's not the only great dish in this bistro, which was founded in 1935. The braised lamb shanks, the chicken with rice and sauce suprême, and the steak tartar are all worth it, not to mention the exquisite tarte Tatin (flambéed with Calvados, of course). The service is old-fashioned and homely, which is perfectly in keeping with the rest. The prices are good given the quality of the produce and the generous portions. The hungry night owls have made this place their favorite spot!

➡ **La Poule au pot**
9, rue Vauvilliers, 75001
Phone: 01 42 36 32 96
M° Les Halles
www.lapouleaupot.com

Closed on Monday and for lunchtime every day. Open until 5am.

● Menu at 40€
● Free choice for about 60€

AU BASCOU

Turbigo – €€€€ | Large tables – Cassoulet

You have arrived in the Kingdom of Basque cooking: this is the terminus, where everybody comes! The décor has a discreet charm, and you could easily go by without noticing it if it weren't for the green front windows, the old-fashioned sign that promotes the "best bistro of the year", and the aromas of southwest France that waft on to the street. The southern sun has been shining here for a few decades. One chef left, but another arrived quickly (the wise and talented Bertrand Guéneron).

It's just as good as it used to be – maybe it's even better. You'll eat the best *piperade* in the city here, a southwestern boudin with Espelette pepper, chestnut soup, and a cassoulet that is beyond reproach (served all year long). The menu changes with the seasons, but is always attached to this particular region, and is virtuosic at reproducing classics from the repertoire: the hare *à la royale* during the game season is wonderful. The produce is selected with care, and is all from the Basque region. If your head is full of Parisian fog, here's a remedy. Choose to eat at the counter or at one of the tables nearby, which are nicer than the ones further down in the room.

CHEZ JANOU

Marais – €€€€ | Provençal food – Terrace

Chez Janou is the remedy for Provence natives who miss their region. This place plays the southern card (maybe too much): pastis everywhere (over 80 different types are listed), olives as an aperitif, movie posters for *César*, *Le Schpountz* and *Manon des Sources* on the walls, yellow everywhere, a shaded terrace, and olive-trees in pots.

What can you do? You have to give the southerners back their smiles! Their Proustian madeleine is tapenade, anchoïade, ratatouille, fried smelts, vegetable tian, rabbit confit, and cod brandade. The must-eat provençal *petits farcis* made by Janou are certainly not the best you'll have in your life, but they are good enough to satisfy your need for sun, and that's already something. Add the effortless service, a few Japanese and American tourists, and you will experience southern nonchalance as if you were in Provence, complete with the accent, too.

➡️ Au Bascou
38, rue Réaumur, 75003
Phone: 01 42 72 69 25
M° Arts-et-Métiers
www.au-bascou.fr

Closed on Saturday and Sunday

● Lunch set menu for 18€
● Dinner set menus from 36€ to 60€
● Free choice for about 45€

➡️ Chez Janou
2, rue Roger-Verlomme, 75003
Phone: 01 42 72 28 41
M° Chemin-Vert
www.chezjanou.com

Open every day

● Lunch set menu for 14.50€
● Free choice between 30€ and 40€

× **CHEZ JANOU** ×

Chez Janou: it's pastis everywhere, tapenade, and ratatouille!
The cooking, the terrace, and the olive trees should satisfy your need for the sun.

L'AUBERGE BRESSANE
Champ de Mars – €€€€ | Small terrace

At L'Auberge Bressane, you'll go back in time and learn a three-part lesson in French history. First of all there's the setting, which looks like a tavern from the Middle Ages: everything is made of wood, the seats are hobnailed, there are hunting pictures on the walls, the tablecloths and wallpaper are ornate with lilies, and there are charcuterie diplomas and wrought-iron lamps. This décor doesn't care for trends, and is a bastion against modernity. Second, the ambiance is dimmed and warm; the wait staff are dressed in black and white and run around efficiently as the boss looks on; tourists are happy to have found such a place, and plenty of regulars and *bon vivants* party without restraint.

Finally, there is the strong traditional cooking. For nostalgic people from Lyon, there are the fish quenelles; for Francophiles, the frog *persillade*; for gourmets, the sweetbread with morels and the sole *meunière*. Sauces, seasonal game, homemade desserts (wonderful soufflés and must-eat crepes Suzettes), Burgundy and Beaujolais wines to drown it all. The lunch menu is reasonably priced; for the rest, you will pay a price for quality produce and a nice setting. Keep it in mind to warm you up on cold days of nostalgia.

➧ **L'Auberge bressane**
16, avenue de La Motte-Picquet, 75007
Phone: 01 47 05 98 37
M° La Tour-Maubourg
or École-Militaire
www.auberge-bressane.com

Closed for lunch on Saturday

● Lunch set menu for 24.50€
● Sunday set menu at 29.50€
● Free choice between 40€ and 60€

CAFÉ DES ABATTOIRS
Place Vendôme – €€€€ | Counter – For meat-eaters

The name, which means "Slaughterhouse Café", leaves little to the imagination. The ladies of the Rostang dynasty have made it their mission to modernize this meat-eaters' bistro, and they weren't afraid to break old habits. The décor is contemporary, with leather on the walls, and the food is amazing: variety meats are given special treatment, and the kitchen offers rakish dishes.

On the menu: meat. Before being able to taste the rib steak from Brittany (super tender and deliciously smoked – it's cooked in a wood-oven), or the ox tripe gratin from Lyon (much less fat than you can imagine), before eating a veal tartar from Limousin with Caesar sauce (all sauces, BBQ, tarragon etc. are homemade), or eating the fries that accompany the spatchcocked young cockerel, you will have to share appetizers placed on the table (pumpkin soup, lentil salad, scrambled eggs, and shrimp fritter). Consider this a way to encourage camaraderie. Nice produce, nice cooking, generosity: there is no doubt that things are done well here. The service is efficient and cheerful, just like the clientele from this chic but not uptight neighborhood. For the aperitif: nice wines and divine snacks.

➡ **Café des Abattoirs**
10, rue Gomboust, 75001
Phone: 01 76 21 77 60
M° Pyramides
www.cafedesabattoirs.com

Open every day

● Lunch set menu for 22€
● Dinner set menus at 32€, 38€ or 45€

LE ROI DU POT-AU-FEU

Madeleine — €€€€

This is what we call an atmospheric bistro. Can you get the best *pot-au-feu* in Paris here? There's no point in debating it: not only is the dish well executed, made with good produce, and with respect for grand tradition, but also, it's not even the only dish that has made the reputation of this place. You have to see it to believe it: a tiny restaurant with checkered tablecloths, ancient tiles, a large bar, unique wine pitchers (the côte roannaise is billed *à la ficelle*), and lost Japanese tourists. It's been open for forty years, non-stop, all day.

If you feel like having some cold meats at 4pm, or a warm soup, a marrowbone, some pâté or, of course, the famous *pot-au-feu*, this is where you should go. You will be welcomed and served efficiently, and with energy. The menu is quite short, but does offer alternatives to the star dish (shepherd's pie, rib steak...) as well as simple, delicious homemade desserts. But they're not really the reason we go there.

➡ **Le Roi du pot-au-feu**
34, rue Vignon, 75009
Phone: 01 47 42 37 10
M° Havre-Caumartin
or Madeleine

Closed on Sunday, non-stop service in the afternoon

● *Pot-au-feu* for 18€
● Free choice around 25€

AUBERGE PYRÉNÉES CÉVENNES

République – €€€€
Tablier de sapeur and incredible cassoulet

If you're the kind of person who likes modern bistros with stripped-down décor and innovative food, you can skip this page. Checkered tablecloths, saucissons hanging from the ceiling, large beams, hunting trophies, small wooden chairs... here, all of this tends to create a rustic and warm atmosphere, which the jovial and friendly service only emphasizes.

On the menu, the chef's heart is balanced between the wonders of Lyon specialties and the delights of southwestern cuisine. Frisée salad with lardons, pan-fried calves' liver, duck confit, cassoulet (which lives up to its reputation as the best in all Paris), duck breast, sweetbreads, fish quenelles... Heavy stuff! Adventurous types will find specialties here that they can't find anywhere else in Paris, like the *tablier de sapeur* and warm pistachio saucisson. The portions are generous and the food good, and can be served alone or as part of a set menu (30.25€) reserved for *bon vivants*. In order to have enough space left to eat the delicious profiteroles after all that, you'll need a champion stomach.

➡ **Auberge Pyrénées Cévennes**
106, rue de la Folie-Méricourt, 75011
Phone: 01 43 57 33 78
M° Goncourt or Parmentier

Closed for lunch on Saturday, and all day Sunday

● Menu for 30.25€
● Free choice between 35€ and 50€

CHEZ FRED

Péreire – €€€€ | Valet

Things were starting to get a little boring at Chez Fred. Thankfully, this bistro is back on the right track now. It is one of the best Parisian bistros when it comes to Lyonnais specialties. It has been on boulevard Pereire since 1945, and still has timeless charm. The décor features the famous Lyon characters Guignol and Gnafron (you can't escape clichés), as well as essentials of the genre: big mirrors, old tiles, an impressive hat collection, nice bistro furniture, competent and jovial service, and white aprons. At the table, things flow naturally (and so does the Beaujolais wine).

The menu changes regularly, but the dishes are always made for bold spirits, big Lyonnais appetites, and people who aren't scared of eating a lot. Some entrées are thankfully available all the time: the iconic

tablier de sapeur, fish quenelles, potatoes and herrings *à l'huile* (the pot is brought on the table), warm pistachio saucisson, huge éclairs, or praline tarts. We've finally found the authentic spirit of Lyon in the north of Paris!

LE QUINCY

Gare de Lyon – €€€€

Le Quincy is a world in itself. First, there is the décor: woodwork, checkered tablecloths, knick-knacks accumulated over time, and funny messages ("Don't yell at the boss, his wife will do it for you!", "To a paunch, nothing is impossible!"). This bistro is for nostalgic swaggerers, for Parisians that miss the warmth and solidity of the province.

Second, there is the menu composed of robust dishes (at robust prices) from the past and from home, with an inclination for specialties from the Berry and Ardèche regions. A giant stuffed cabbage you can cut like a cake, an iconic *blanquette*, an impeccable *pot-au-feu*, and crawfish you can watch in the aquarium before seeing it in your plate. It is all delicious, and plentiful. At Quincy, the food is not made for small eaters and bird-like appetites!

Third and last, there is Bobosse, the boss. There are people he just doesn't like, and you'd better not be one of them! If he likes you, though (and to be certain he likes you, we suggest you come on a motorbike – he loves motorbikes), you are sure to spend one hell of an evening. A piece of advice: end your meal with the flambéed plums (this gives way to a show that's either rejoicing or pathetic – we can't decide). Don't forget your checkbook; this house doesn't take credit cards. We told you it would take you to another world!

➡ **Chez Fred**
190 *bis*, boulevard Pereire, 75017
Phone: 01 45 74 20 48
M° Argentine

Closed on Saturday and Sunday

● Free choice for about 50€

➡ **Le Quincy**
28, avenue Ledru-Rollin, 75012
Phone: 01 46 28 46 76
M° Ledru-Rollin
www.lequincy.fr

Closed on Saturday, Sunday and Monday

● Free choice for about 60€

× **CHEZ FRED** ×

In this Parisian bistro serving specialties from Lyon, the timeless charm, pistachio saucisson, and huge éclairs will not disappoint even the largest appetites!

ATELIER VIVANDA

Étoile – €€€€

This place is the realization of the starred chef Akrame Benallal's carnivorous dream: a stall dedicated to meat-eating. Everything has been conceived by a meat-loving mind in this tiny bistro (which can seat 24 people, and is always full): you will eat meat on butcher's chopping blocks underneath the gaze of the cow on the wall (rest assured – they're just photographs), while the nice waitress serves you dressed in a leather apron. Nice pieces of beef and chicken hang from the kitchen walls.

There is only one menu option: appetizer, entrée, and dessert for 35€. The food is of great quality in the bistro-meat repertoire: mimosa eggs mayonnaise with mustard, Black Angus beef (but you can also get chicken, veal, or duck) which is tender and perfectly cooked, served with parsley, gratin dauphinois, dauphine potato (tanned, crusty, and creamy, so rare in Paris), homemade mash, or darphin potatoes. The chef pays attention to details here, and even made an Italian peppered olive oil which enhances the taste of the meat without overpowering it: superb! (Yes, you can actually add olive oil to your meat here – no judgment.) Last pleasant surprise: the clientele is surprisingly feminine... you don't say!

➡ **Atelier Vivanda**
18, rue Lauriston, 75016
Phone: 01 40 67 10 00
M° Kléber or Charles-de-Gaulle-Étoile
www.ateliervivanda.com
Two other addresses:
82, rue des Archives, 75003,
and 20, rue du Cherche-Midi, 75006

Closed on Saturday and Sunday

● Menu for 35€

LA POINTE DU GROUIN

Gare du Nord – €€€€ | Tapas from Brittany

In the small rue Belzunce, you will find the quiet bistro Chez Michel, where the impeccable food is made up of specialties from Brittany; Chez Casimir, the wooden bistro where the best brunch in all of Paris is served (made in Breizh as well), and La Pointe du Grouin, an Armorican bistro. Thierry Breton heads this empire of three bistros (with a name like that, what else could he do?) We can't decide which one you should go to first – they all have their own mood and are recommendable for different things. But if you're not afraid of sharing a table with strangers, if you like noise and the whirlwind of life, try out La Pointe du Grouin. You will first need to exchange your euros into the local

currency – the grouin – before ordering at the counter. After a few minutes, your name will be shouted out and you can come get your order.

In the evening, you can drink cider, wine, or a good Philomenn while treating yourself to delicious tapas (around 6€). We recommend the sausage galette, the charcuterie platter, and the wonderful homemade boudin, the kouign-amann cake, and the goose neck barnacles when they're available. You'll see for yourself the other delights on the menu. For lunch, this is a great place to eat, with 4€ sandwiches.

➡ La Pointe du Grouin
8, rue de Belzunce, 75010
No phone number
M° Gare-du-Nord
wwwlapointedugroin.com

**Open every day,
late closing time**

● Free choice, between 4€ and 15€ for lunch, up to 30€ for dinner

LE TERROIR PARISIEN

Maubert – €€€€ | Large tables – Counter

The idea behind this place is simple: in this bistro, Yannick Alléno and his three stars bend over backwards to celebrate Parisian produce and iconic recipes. This is not an excuse to be old-fashioned: the checkered tablecloths, moleskin banquettes, and outdated woodwork have not been asked to stay. In his 5th arrondissement annexe (the other address is at the foot of palais Brongniart), this great chef preferred a chic and contemporary décor. The story is told through the food here.

On the menu, you will find Parisian classics – sometimes forgotten recipes like Crécy broth, Halles gratin, or jellied eggs *à la froufrou*... And so as not to do things by halves (Alléno is not that kind of cook), he makes sure the produce is local. The asparagus come from Argenteuil, the charcuterie from the 6th arrondissement (Gilles Vérot), the beans from Arpagon... The result is astonishing. The plates that are put in front of you are like Parisian women: elegant and impish. To do better than New Yorkers, try the revised hog-dog *veau chaud*, with a veal sausage and gribiche sauce. Our favorite spot is, as always, at the counter.

➡ Le Terroir parisien
20, rue Saint-Victor, 75005
Phone: 01 44 31 54 54
M° Maubert-Mutualité
www.yannick-alleno.com
Other address: 25, place de la Bourse, 75002

Open every day

● Free choice around 30€

THE NEW GUARD

Those who say French gastronomy is dead are obviously blind, or have burnt their tongue on a liquid nitrogen dish. Believe us, we've never eaten better in Paris than we do now.

There isn't a single month that goes by without a wonderful new eaterie opening up on the streets of Paris. Not a week passes when a restaurant doesn't open down the block from you that you'd like to make your daily canteen. There's not one kitchen among the "gourmet restaurants" that hasn't lost a young, promising, and extremely talented chef who wants to open up his or her own bistro.

This general movement is not only taking place in the bohemian quarters of northeast Paris – it even takes place in the richest parts of the city. Young chefs with CVs as long as rhubarb are here to take care of your appetite. They are here with young hearts, ready to give themselves entirely to their work, and to spoil a clientele that is rushing back, once more, to restaurants.

They are the future of bistros, perhaps even the future of cooking. Let them handle your lunches, friendly or romantic dinners, your small hungers and big appetites. That's all they're waiting for.

LES AFFRANCHIS

Pigalle – €€€€

These Goodfellas (the restaurant is named after the French title of the movie) have never played in a Scorsese movie, but their CVs are bulletproof nonetheless. This nice neo-bistro on the hills of the 9th arrondissement, with a few mirrors on the walls, homemade pickles on the counter, and jazz music playing in the background, is the work of two chefs just out of L'Ambroisie (a three-star Place des Vosges). In here, the cooking is done with four hands – Enrico Bertazzo's (he's Italian) and Keenan Ballois (he's not Irish) – and they are four very capable hands!

The recipe is effective: simple produce, gourmet techniques, traditions explored and modernized (but not too much), juices, sauces, and bases with real flavor. Everything we love is here. The food is gourmet and refined without making a fuss. Don't miss the veal cheek, which is prepared for two days and is both melting and spicy; or the carbonara-style egg cooked at low temperature, which caresses its lardons voluptuously. You won't risk being robbed here either, as lunch costs around 30€ and dinner 40€. These Goodfellas won't stay undercover for long.

➡ **Les Affranchis**
5, rue Henry-Monnier, 75009
Phone: 01 45 26 26 30
M° Saint-Georges

Closed on Monday

● Lunch set menus for 28€ or 32€
● Dinner for 40€

L'ESQUISSE

Marcadet – €€€€

On the hills of Montmartre, this bistro may look like many others, with its wooden tables and metal industrial chairs, its large room that opens out onto a counter with a huge chalkboard, and its open kitchen where two young women work calmly. A food safe, shelves, homemade cans, wine cartons lying around... it's a pleasant mess, just like life. In a corner on the floor, the chalkboard will reassure you: goat cheese panna cotta, beetroot, thyme-lemon granite, lean meat with licorice, patty pan squash gratin; pigs' feet fries, parsnip mash and hot mayo; mint-chocolate After Eight coffee... Simple and delightful produce, creativity and generosity: all the rules of good bistronomy are respected here. This will make any old-time flavor fans happy. And not just them.

Vivacity, *gourmandise*, and happiness are on the menu here. The young chef Laetitia Bret (who used to work at the Bistral and the Ritz) has a pronounced taste for surprises and mixing genres. Thomas Meunier takes care of the room and the wines, and excels at finding wonderful little bottles. The pricing is respectful in these hard times. To sum up, this is a local place just as we like them, particularly in its kindness and heart-warming ways.

CORETTA

Batignolles – €€€€

Often, the tiniest of things can brighten up a neighborhood deserted by restaurants. In the Cardinet quarter, which is brand new and rather cold, a resplendent neo-bistro called Coretta has brought light to the entire street. A trio from Neva (a nice place near Saint-Lazare) manages this place, and the chefs, Beatriz Gonzalez and Jean-François Pantaleon, used to work at La Grande Cascade. Everything is exciting here: the duplex contemporary and eco-sustainable décor brightens the night-time glow and sparkles in the daylight. The welcome and the service show the true enthusiasm that only generous and honest restaurants can have.

The plates mix neo-bourgeois audacity with gourmet restaurant precision. The sweetbread is crisp and melting, the striped ray combines beautifully with pig feet, pak choï and black garlic; and the white pear is perfumed with verbena. It's brilliant, and sinfully good. The wine list offers well-chosen and original drinks (try the wines from Vendée). The neighborhood regulars mix with foodies that come from all four corners of the city. Because yes, Coretta is the kind of place you could, and should, cross Paris for.

➡️ **L'Esquisse**
151 *bis*, rue Marcadet, 75018
Phone: 01 53 41 63 04
M° Lamarck-Caulaincourt

**Closed on Sunday
and Monday**

● Lunch menu between 17€ and 22€
● Free choice between 30€ and 40€

➡️ **Coretta**
151 *bis*, rue Cardinet, 75017
Phone: 01 42 26 55 55
M° Brochant

Closed Sunday

● Lunch set menus for 24€, 33€ and 39€

× **CORETTA** ×
In this resplendent neo-bistro with contemporary and eco-sustainable décor,
you will eat neo-bourgeois cuisine worthy of the best restaurants. An unexpected godsend.

PIROUETTE

Étienne-Marcel – €€€€ | Terrace – Wine to go

For a romantic dinner, a friendly dinner with plenty of drinks, a sunlit lunch on the terrace, to treat your parents, to impress your boss... we'd find all the excuses in the world to taste the food in this place, which does everything right. It is hidden in the Halles forest, on an isolated street. The décor is appealing and airy with bright wood, lights, and glass. The wine list is large and features wonderful bottles. And the food...

Chef Tomy Gousset mixes precision, elegance, and creativity. The dinner menu is 42€, but what a menu! Egg parfait with chestnut-mushroom velouté, mullet, salsify and meat juices, mango tart... He never runs out of inspiration, and the food is just as good as it looks. Fish, meat, vegetables, cheese, dessert: everything spins the right way. Gourmets on a budget will enjoy the 20€ lunch menu, which deserves an ovation.

➡ **Pirouette**
5, rue Mondétour, 75001
Phone: 01 40 26 47 81
M° Étienne-Marcel
www.oenolis.com/pirouette

Closed on Sunday

● Lunch set menu for 20€
● Dinner menus between 42€ and 62€

ZÉBULON

Palais-Royal – €€€€ | Table d'hôte – Wine cellar

The team from Pirouette has opened this modern, clear, and spacious bistro to replace the old Pierre in Palais-Royal, which used to switch hands often without ever truly finding its way. All of today's trends are exemplified here: wine cellar, open kitchen, table d'hôtes, nice colors, and vintage furniture. The head chef, Yannick Lahopgnou, is from Cameroun and worked for Alléno at Meurice before moving to Osaka.

Full of talent, he offers an honest and strong cuisine: he isn't afraid to satisfy large appetites, knows how to make amazing sauces, and adds a touch of Asian influences to his dishes (we mentioned Osaka)! For example, the beef featherblade steak with pan-fried parsnip, candied shallots, and shimeji tempura, which is valiant and different, or the fennel turbot with a little nori seaweed. The wines are quite good (although you should expect to pay 7 to 15€ for a glass), and you can buy them in the wine cellar next-door and bring your own. This beautiful place is for solid appetites, and offers plates with a twist that can send you sky high (just like the prices, except the set lunch menu).

CAILLEBOTTE

Martyrs – €€€€ | Counter

This place pays homage to the painter who illustrated the construction of Saint-Lazare station at the end of the nineteenth century. Gustave Caillebotte was caught between the Impressionist and Modernist movements, with one foot in tradition and another in modernity. This is the perfect description for this bistro, where Franck Baranger (a very talented chef, formerly at the Bristol and who also works for Pantruche) and Edouard Bobin (who walks with discreet elegance among the tables) mix these two features with dexterity. The cooking is creative and bright, but it is also anchored in strong traditions and in the expertise of gourmet restaurants.

As at Pantruche, the food is precise: it's not just about throwing some great ingredients on to a plate – here, the chef knows how to really cook them. The cheerful inspiration of the service will make you feel at home immediately. The red beetroot soup (from the family garden) with fresh goat cheese and fish eggs is a delicate, bright red dish. The roasted veal with parsnip mousse and Jerusalem artichoke crisps is a tender and light Autumn dish. The décor is bright and verdant with a Nordic simplicity, the trendy kitchen opens onto the main room and there are a few seats at the bar for lunch, which are – it goes without saying – our favorites.

➡ **Zébulon**
10, rue de Richelieu, 75001
Phone: 01 42 36 49 44
M° Palais-Royal-Musée du Louvre
www.oenolis.com/zebulon-palaisroyal

Closed on Sunday

● Lunch menus at 20€ and 45€

➡ **Caillebotte**
8, rue Hippolyte-Lebas, 75009
Phone: 01 53 20 88 70
M° Notre-Dame-de-Lorette

Closed on Saturday and Sunday

● Light lunch set menu for 18€
● Daily special for 14€
● Menu for 34€

JADIS

Convention – €€€€ | Frogs' legs

There are bistros that love to attract revelers, scandal, and crowds. Others are more subtle and discreet, and there reigns a storm-free endless calm. Jadis is hidden in the 15th arrondissement, behind a red-brick frontage, and clearly belongs to the second type. Don't snooze at the décor which is modest, vintage, and iron-clad sober. You'll risk going through a rather sudden wake-up call when you taste the incredible food.

Guillaume Delage learned cooking in Aveyron with Michel Bras. He has chosen to honor the flavors of the past, but not without modernity, technique, and accuracy. Bistro classics are delicately revisited, and sinfully well-made. For those who want to taste everything (we understand), you can also order tapas versions of the entrées. Frogs' legs with soft garlic, melting veal *blanquette* (the house specialty), rum, coffee, and lemon baba... The atmosphere will warm up throughout the meal, with your efficient and generous waiter. The bill is fair (the full menu for 32€) and the wine, well-chosen, will not ruin the appeasing mood.

➡ **Jadis**
208, rue de la Croix-Nivert, 75015
Phone: 01 45 57 73 20
M° Convention
www.bistrotjadisparis.com

Closed on Saturday and Sunday

● Full menu for 32€
● Free choice between 40 and 50€

LE BISTROT BELHARA

Invalides – €€€€

After years of good and loyal service at Bistro Volnay, Thierry Dufroux has set down his saucepans in this pretty neighborhood bistro, where the wealthy clientele of the left bank visit him each day. The décor is warm with provincial charm, cement tiles, red velvet seats, and a bar. In the evening, it lights up with candles and white tablecloths to create a cozy atmosphere.

On the plate, the food is made with a generous and skillful spirit, learned from the best (Guérard, Loiseau, and Ducasse). It's comforting and gourmet. Between a ham platter and a pan-fried boudin, served when they are ready, and a rice pudding with dried fruit, don't miss the house specialty: a warm duck and foie gras pâté (made with seasonal game), crisp and warm like the body of a beautiful sleeping girl. The service has been the same since the beginning, and hasn't lost anything in quality over the years.

WILL

Bastille-Gare de Lyon – €€€€ | Terrace

William Pradeleix had many adventures before opening up this place. He traveled and worked in the most prestigious kitchens (he was Hélène Darroze's sous-chef in London). Since he settled down at this neighborhood bistro that bends the rules by mixing Scandinavian furniture and bright green, this young chef works hard at making meticulous food that is full of character and exotic flavors. Will is the bistro that looks toward Asia, and is always ready to go on an adventure!

Very precise and cooked sublimely, the flavors play with tradition and welcome influences from other continents. Carpaccios seasoned with ginger, pig breast with teriyaki juice, nashi pear-infused shrimp, sea bream with daikon risotto... The trip is spicy, incredibly fresh, and knows how to accommodate flavors. When springtime comes and the sun is out, you can enjoy the terrace and the life around Aligre market. The evening meal is expensive (menu for 45€), but the light lunch set, which includes two appetizers and an entrée for 19€, is a must-eat.

➡ **Le Bistrot Belhara**
23, rue Duvivier, 75007
Phone: 01 45 51 41 77
M° École-Militaire
or La Tour-Maubourg
www.bistrotbelhara.com

Closed on Sunday and Monday

● Lunch set menu at 22.30€
● Dinner set menus at 35€ and 50€

➡ **Will**
75, rue Crozatier, 75012
Phone: 01 53 17 02 44
M° Ledru-Rollin

Closed on Sunday and Monday

● Light lunch for 19€
● Dinner tasting menu for 45€
● Free choice around 50€

× **LE BISTROT BELHARA** ×
A cozy atmosphere with generous food, made with talent.
The chef's specialty: warm duck and foie gras pâté!

× **ROCA** ×

In this bistro, with stone on the walls and black tables, lamb is combined with Japanese seaweed, and gingerbread milk with scallops. Lively, bright, intelligent, and surprising.

LE SERVAN

Voltaire – €€€€ | Counter

When Tatiana Levha, the wife of one of the most popular chefs of recent times (Bertrand Grébaut from Septime) opened up her own restaurant, she got everyone's attention. And when she was joined by her sister and revealed an impressive CV (she worked with Alain Passard and Pascal Barbot), what was mere curiosity became a furious desire to eat there.

The décor is minimal, unoriginal, a typical east Paris look: it seems as though scraping down the walls of an old bistro, varnishing the counter, and not putting a sign out is now the definition of chic modernism. The ceilings are stucco and painted with a pastel sky. The service is sometimes a bit slow, but we'll focus instead on the good food and the nice things Tatiana has accomplished. The plates are full of her talent. They show subtle harmony between flavors (white asparagus, tandoori cream, and fried sage), impeccable cooking, refined mixtures (lacquered pig breast with rhubarb pepper), nice presentation. Flowers and delicacy are everywhere. This young chef will go far. She has enough know-how to get away with the small lunch menu (you get a choice of two dishes only), which is priced nonetheless very reasonably. It's the best deal here at Servan, as prices tend to go way up in the evening.

➡ **Le Servan**
32, rue Saint-Maur, 75011
Phone: 01 55 28 51 82
M° Rue Saint-Maur
leservan.com

Closed on Saturday, Sunday and for lunch on Monday

● Lunch menu at 23€
● In the evening, free choice between 50€ and 60€

A NOSTE

Bourse – €€€€ to €€€€
Tapas – Large tables – Private room available

Between Bourse and Grands Boulevards, this is a place that shows great ambition. To celebrate the cooking of the Landes region, Julien Duboué (who used to be a chef at Afaria) is ready to do anything. In a modern and luminous space filled with blue seats, yellow armchairs, and wine bottles, he unveils the southwestern gourmet Holy Trinity: street food, tapas, and high-end tables. For those in a rush, get a *taloa* – a warm galette, generously garnished – from the food truck. Those who take time to enjoy life will sit at the large tables on the ground floor. With loud laughter, they will share

large, inspired plates. And while they drink, the fine gourmets will slip upstairs to the first floor. Away from the noise, they will enjoy delicate and smart recipes that play with flavors and intensify the produce.

There's no menu here, but a magical set menu for 38€ (60€ in the evening) where you will find the best grilled meat, served in an all-you-can-eat style. That trilogy is unusual, but it works!

ROCA

Porte de Champerret – €€€€

We knew Alexandre Giesbert (the son of... but do we really care?) for his delicious and organic GreenPizz and his rapid time in Richer's kitchens. Here he is, now managing his own bistro with a chic and contemporary décor, grated stone, black tables, and beautiful ceiling lights.

The food is lively, bright, smart, and surprising, because this guy isn't afraid of anything: putting Japanese seaweed underneath lamb, putting corn cream on a low-temperature egg, adding pistachio and wood sorrel oil to a black mullet ceviche, mixing scallops with nut and citrus gingerbread... And it works! Wine-wise, Julien Ross's selection doesn't lag behind. If we add that Alexandre and Julien are adorable and that you can eat there for 20€ or less, you'll understand that you need to book your table, now!

➡ **A Noste**
6 *bis*, rue du 4-Septembre, 75002
Phone: 01 47 03 91 91
M⁰ Bourse
www.a-noste.com

Open every day

● *Taloa* for 6.50€, tapas between 6€ and 19€
● Lunch set menu for 38€
● Dinner set menu for 60€

➡ **Roca**
31, rue Guillaume-Tell, 75017
Phone: 01 47 64 86 04
M° Pereire
www.rocaparis.com

Closed on Saturday and Sunday

● Lunch set menu at 19€
● Free choice between 30€ and 50€

BOUILLON

Trudaine – €€€€

This Bouillon has nothing to do with the restaurants of the same name in the 19th century. It actually draws inspiration from home cooking, with a tendency toward calves' head and guinea fowl with cabbage. Marc Favier used to be Jean-François Piège's sous-chef, and he set up a repertoire which sways between tradition and originality in this small, only lightly decorated restaurant south of Pigalle.

On the menu, with a slight southwestern accent, the bohemian, chic clientele of the 9th mingles with big eaters, and they can practice their knowledge of modern bistro classics: whole duck from Maison Burgaud with small potatoes, or the now iconic koka *pissaladière*. You will always find a wonderful broth on the menu as well, like the one made with Parisian mushrooms, foie gras, celery, coriander, and smoked vinegar. Marc Favier imported from fancy neighborhoods the love of good produce, and it's a particular attention to gleaming vegetables that give the plates a party glow. It is fresh, it is pretty, and the 14€ daily special is a very good deal.

➡ Bouillon
47, rue de Rochechouart, 75009
Phone: 09 51 18 66 59
M° Poissonnière or Anvers

Closed on Sunday and Monday

● Daily special for 14€
● Free choice between 40€ and 50€

LE GALOPIN

Belleville – €€€€ | Large tables

At the head of this bistro, located near the pretty place Sainte-Marthe, you will find Romain Tischenko (winner of Top Chef 2010) and his brother. Inside, a space that can fit 20 people, with rough stone walls and wooden tables. In this modest (not to say common), décor a unique menu is served every night for 54€, composed of seven dishes that vary according to the season and the chef's inspiration.

The cooking is creative and sophisticated, and likes to surprise customers by playing with flavors (during winter, the fish is cooked with mandarins), textures, and appearances, and by rehabilitating forgotten *fumets* with today's techniques. For lunch, you can make up your full menu (32€) by choosing between entrées. Here again, fresh market produce allow for a refined and ingenious cuisine. Even though this bistro

➡ Le Galopin
34, rue Sainte-Marthe, 75010
Phone: 01 42 06 05 03
M° Belleville or Goncourt
www.le-galopin.com

Closed for lunch on Monday, Tuesday and Wednesday; closed all day Saturday and Sunday

● For lunch, full menu at 32€
● For dinner, tasting menu at 54€

is quite expensive (especially when you compare it to the standard prices in this neighborhood), it will nonetheless find a way to make your life sweeter. The service gives information and advice generously, and the natural wine list is good. For large families or large groups of friends, there are big tables in the basement.

GARE AU GORILLE

Batignolles — €€€€

This is a story of transmission. The chef at Gare au Gorille learned to cook with Alain Passard (l'Arpège) and was sous-chef of Bertrand Grébaut (Septime). In this new bistro in Batignolles, you will find the half-rough, half-sophisticated ambiance that's very in right now: untreated wood, naked light bulbs, opinel knives, candles with Flemish perfumes, and immaculate tiles on the floor...

At the end of the long main room, the kitchen shines bright. That's where the delicate and refined dishes come from. For lunch and for 25€ (pinch us!), you can taste the subtle and unexpected balance of delicate and translucent compositions (thin slices of raw veal on a herring purée with leek, sliced radish, and crisp croutons; cod with watercress purée, large cabbage leaves, Romanesco, and, hidden underneath, a piece of lardo di Colonnata). This food should be tasted and enjoyed.

The wine list playfully unveils natural bottles, among others, which are well chosen, as well as a surprising selection of Greek wines. We have one regret: the super-short menu for lunch only gives you two choices between meat or fish. It's a little slim.

➡ **Gare au gorille**
68, rue des Dames, 75017
Phone: 01 42 94 24 02
M° Rome

Closed on Sunday and Monday

● Lunch menu for 25€
● For dinner, prices range from 30€ to 50€

Nicolas Chatenier's
VIEW ON BISTROS
—◆—

General associate at Grandes Tables du Monde

We're in 1965 in Asnières, close to Gennevilliers, in a rather shady industrial neighborhood. A bistro in liquidation has just found a new owner. The chef's name is Michel Guérard. He was a pastry chef at Crillon hotel. He bought the place for nothing, because he promised his parents he would settle. He names the bistro Le Pot-au-feu.

Within a few months, this shady spot became the place where all Parisians went. Régine, Ted Kennedy, Alain Delon, and Mireille Darc, they all found their way to this old bistro where you enter through the service courtyard. The place is banal, it can barely hold thirty people, but the cooking is brilliant. Guérard cooks "like the bird sings". Chicken wings mix with cucumber; raw foie gras seasons the famous gourmet salad; pears find refuge underneath caramelized puff pastry. Guérard takes a step away from traditional techniques to invent a new style of French cooking. This is how he launched a career that would earn him two Michelin stars in 1977.

When, in 1992, nearly thirty years later, chef Yves Camdeborde left Crillon hotel to move to Porte d'Orléans, he was doing exactly the same thing: with little money, he took his bistro to an unpopular neighborhood on the edge of the city. The success was immediate and paved the way for generations of cooks, like Eric Fréchon, who won three stars and opened La Verrière in 1995 at Buttes-Chaumont.

The bistro is a generous kind of cooking, which brings the most talented chefs out of high-end gourmet restaurants to create their own establishments, and meet fame. The bistro is the antechamber of the greatest chefs.

CHIC BISTROS

We could judge them (too hastily) as too nice, with their white tablecloths, sparkling silverware, and manicured décor that looks like it came from an upscale apartment. We could worry about getting bored there, with a food routine of lamb-flageolets, foie gras, and grandma's desserts. We could expect bad service with a military feel about it. We would be wrong.

In Paris, a chic bistro could very well surprise you. It's not because it looks nice and clean that it can't mess with old customs. It brings you a heavy dose of calories, leaves generous and playful dishes on your table, slips into your mouth the richness of a vol-au-vent, or the malice of a roasted chicken with dignified origins.

What can we say? Beauty attracts us. A well laid-out table, a stylish décor, vintage from the 1950s, very contemporary or gilded... all of this draws us in, and, some days, enchants us. Tables with enough space between them to allow pleasant conversation. A full wine list that takes you on a trip as you turn the pages. No familiarity. All of these details denote the peaceful atmosphere of a well-bred bistro.

Do you crave a little luxury, calm, and delight too? Here, just for you, is our selection of the Parisian tables that have good manners.

BENOIT

Hôtel de Ville – €€€€

This bistro is over 100 years old (it opened in 1912) and it is the prototype of the French bistro as seen in American movies like Woody Allen's. The décor is made up of copper and engraved glasses, a wooden bar, Italian tiles, red velvet banquettes, fake marble columns, and black-and-white, friendly service. Like the bourgeois houses of the good old days, it also has white tablecloths and silverware.

On the menu there is traditional cuisine full of panache and generosity, which d'Artagnan or Cyrano wouldn't say no to: one of the best *pâté en croûte* in Paris, exceptional sweetbreads served with foie gras, cockerel crest, and kidney served in a truffle gravy. The Lucullus veal tongue chitchats with the nantua sole filet. Cassoulet is served during the season, along with calves' head in *ravigote* sauce. Escargots with garlic butter and crayfish soup cultivate a healthy nostalgia. The portions are large, the fresh produce carefully chosen (the table is now part of the Ducasse empire), the traditional wine list is deep... in return, of course, the prices go way up at night. If you are lucky and choose well on the menu, you will see the show – threatened with extinction – of real table service.

➤ Benoit
20, rue Saint-Martin, 75004
Phone: 01 58 00 22 05
M° Châtelet or Hôtel-de-Ville
www.benoit-paris.com

Open every day

● Lunch menu at 39€
● Free choice between 70€ and 80€

L'ANTRE AMIS

Breteuil – €€€€ | Terrace

In this neighborhood, good restaurants are quite rare. Thankfully, on the border between the 7th and the 15th arrondissements, this chic bistro, with its strong attachment to the traditions of good hosting, is the right place for knowledgeable gourmets to go. There is only a little space in this neat, classical, and error-free décor. It is refined, goes well with the neighborhood and, although there aren't any white tablecloths on the wooden tables, you will eat with good silverware. Amid this outdated French elegance, the wait staff are loquacious but well behaved.

You will order from a chalkboard that features a unique menu. The cooking is bourgeois, of course. But it uses traditions well to mold delicate and creative

flavors. The plates are generous and the presentation is nice: this all communicates a true love for good things. The hare *à la royale* (during hunting season), chicken supreme, homemade gnocchi, braised beef cheek, and macaroni gratin... the mood doesn't contradict the name of this place, which is a play on words meaning "among friends". True friendliness is born in this soft and discreet setting. Share the delicious food with a good bottle (the list is smart), on the small terrace during hot days.

➡ **L'Antre Amis**
9, rue Bouchut, 75015
Phone: 01 45 67 15 65
Mᵒ Sèvres-Lecourbe
or Ségur
www.lantreamis.com

**Closed on Saturday
and Sunday**

● Menu at 35€

EDGAR

Sentier – €€€€ | Terrace

We could go there just for the terrace, which is well-sized, and situated, like an unexpected gift, in a quiet, secret corner close to Sentier. We could go there for the blue and copper décor, which draws inspiration from sexy/mythical visions of the 1950s...

And we could certainly go there for the superb food. Sea flavors, shellfish, salty perfumes: the sea has found a home here. In the open kitchens, the cooking is perfectly adapted to make small dishes like Roumégous oysters, Qwehli shrimp, razor clams, or jumbo shrimp... The wines are light and easy to drink, and, when the springtime comes, this place is filled with *joie de vivre*. The octopus fricassee with sweet paprika is crisp and tender, and a must-eat. A few meats are offered for lost carnivores.

➡ **Edgar**
31, rue d'Alexandrie, 75002
Phone: 01 40 41 05 69
M° Sentier or Strasbourg-
Saint-Denis
www.edgarparis.com

Open every day

● Daily starter at 8€
● Daily entrée special
at 14€
● Free choice between
30€ and 50€

× **EDGAR** ×
At Edgar's, sea flavors, shellfish, and salty perfumes have found a home.
You will eat in a blue and copper décor with a mythical, sexy 1950s mood.

AUX PRÉS

Saint-Germain-des-Prés – €€€€

As you enter this prosperous bistro near Saint-Germain-des-Prés, you will think: "Am I in Paris? London? New York?" It doesn't matter. Let's say that the long white marble bar (having a seat there by the window is our top choice) reminds us of London cocktail bars; that the floral wallpaper and leather chairs are reminiscent of New York chic; and that the food, well-made by famous chef Cyril Lignac (whose celebrity meant some people forgot that he trained with Ducasse and Passard), twists the French culinary repertoire with talent and enthusiasm.

You have to try the crunchy rice, marinated tuna and avocado, the generous chimichurri beef, and the raspberry French toast, which is simultaneously crisp and melting. On top of all this, the service is vigilant and friendly, and holds this bistro together like a nice, bourgeois house. The clientele is cosmopolitan, so you'll feel pleasantly disoriented. The prices are left bank prices: that's the rule.

➤ Aux Prés
27, rue du Dragon, 75006
Phone: 01 45 48 28 68
M° Saint-Germain-des-Prés
or Saint-Sulpice
www.restaurantauxpres.com

Open every day

● Menus at 32€ and 45€

LE COQ RICO

Lamarck-Caulaincourt – €€€€ | Table d'hôtes

We come to this chic *rotisserie* perched up in Montmartre to dine with the prettiest chicks in town. In Antoine Westermann's brilliant bistro, this serial restaurant-owner celebrates chicken in every possible way, by the bar or on the large table (10 guests at a time don't scare him).

Here, there's no need to choose between the chicken and the egg. On the appetizer menu, the egg is cooked in every possible way and according to each season: mimosa with preserved tuna filets from Lisbon; hard-boiled (our favorite); with salmon and bread strips with seaweed butter; or sunny-side up with smoked breast on a grilled tartine. For the entrée, you can choose between Bresse chicken, guinea fowl from Auvergne, Dombes duckling, red chicken from Vaucluse, Chalans chicken... You can pick a dish on the menu, or choose a whole chicken to share with others. The jus is incredible, the cooking is perfect, and the

sides carefully prepared. For lunch, you can get a daily special for 15€. The rest of the time, the prices are quite high (25€ for an entrée, and between 80 and 100€ for an entire chicken for two to four people); that's not surprising, given they are luxurious chicks.

CHAUMETTE

Auteuil — €€€€ | Covered terrace

This place is next door to Maison de la Radio, so you'll come across all the radio stars! Journalists with recognizable voices come here to enjoy the nostalgic atmosphere, straight from the 1950s.

The décor is purposefully dark, and the film director Claude Autant-Lara would have just loved the chic woodwork, old framed pictures, piles of books, and smart tablecloths. You come here to taste family food that stays true to tradition, and the recipes that have now become grand French legends. For instance: a sinful Rossini tournedos; a remarkable *pot-au-feu*, or a sweetly perfumed navarin of lamb.

Let the attentive and warm service drive you (along with the pleasant lunch set menu) and pick whatever you want: the produce is always carefully chosen, and the chef's technique is perfect. After having paid your dues to the nice wine list, and finished your large plates, will you still be hungry enough to eat a delicious Bourbon vanilla millefeuille? We hope you will be!

➡ **Le Coq Rico**
98, rue Lepic, 75018
Phone: 01 42 59 82 89
www.lecoqrico.com
M° Lamarck-Caulaincourt

**Open every day,
until midnight**

● Daily special at 15€
● Free choice around 50€

➡ **Chaumette**
7, rue Gros, 75016
Phone: 01 42 88 29 27
M° Jasmin
or Javel-André Citroën
www.restaurant-chaumette.com

**Closed for lunch on Saturday,
and all day Sunday**

● Lunch set menu for 25€ (35€ on weekends)
● Dinner menu at 35€
● Free choice for about 40€

× **AUX PRÉS** ×
White marble bar, floral wallpaper, and leather seats in Cyril Lignac's bistro.
In this New Yorker-chic décor, the French culinary repertoire is twisted with talent and enthusiasm.

LES 110 DE TAILLEVENT
Champs-Élysées – €€€€
Counter – Large wine list

Ali Baba had 40 thieves. Taillevent has 110 different wines to taste by the glass. At the corner of rue du Faubourg-Saint-Honoré, the prestigious house opened a luxurious bistro with a wonderful concept: each course on the menu comes with four glasses of wine. The prices rise very quickly (from 5 to 100€), but the wide range and careful selection allow both rich amateurs and more modest fans to pair food and wine beautifully. And you will catch on quickly. Especially because, on the other side of the bar (once more, our favorite spot), the sommelier watches you, and gives precious and wise advice.

Alongside to all these nice bottles, well displayed in the oh-so chic décor of leather, blond wood, and sepia engravings, the food is just as good: French gastronomy is well represented here. The vol-au-vent *à la financière* is undoubtedly the best in Paris, and the beurre blanc turbot or calves' liver on the weekly menu are now iconic. A delightful experience for elegant hedonists, for lunch or for dinner.

Around 1pm, the ambiance is driven by suits and business. After 8pm, by long skirts and secret-sharing. Either way, no one seems shocked by the golden prices.

➡ Les 110 de Taillevent
195, rue du Faubourg-Saint-Honoré, 75008
Phone: 01 40 74 20 20
M° Charles de Gaulle-Étoile
taillevent.com/les-110-de-taillevent-brasserie

Open every day

● For lunch and dinner, 44€ menu
● Free choice around 80€

× **LES 110 DE TAILLEVENT** ×
One hundred and ten, that's the number of wines listed in this place!
In a leather and blond wood setting, gastronomy and *grand crus* wines pair wonderfully.

L'AFFABLE

Rue du Bac – €€€€

The former chef at L'Affable left to open Coretta, a nice restaurant far from the 7th arrondissement and its ministries. It was the young sous-chef, Guillaume Monet, who took over with great ideas and real talent. This gentle and venerable place lives up to its name. The service is joyous, hospitable, and attentive. The décor is inspired by chic and retro bistros (with a counter, red banquettes, cement tiles, and round lamps), and the local bourgeois can enjoy nice homemade dishes, served in large portions and cooked with sensitivity.

The menu changes with the seasons, but consistently offers the classics: frog's legs, crisp sweetbreads with a truffle celery risotto, oxtail ravioli, foie gras with lemongrass vegetable consommé, and passion fruit crème brûlée with biscuits from Brittany. The flavors will surprise you, the cooking is perfect... nothing here is off-key. The wine list is skillfully put together. L'Affable is good, but never boring. If you want to pass yourself of as the perfect son-in-law, this is where you should bring your in-laws. They will be in awe of the wait staffs' good manners, and the finesse and generosity of the food. Meanwhile, try to not look panicked when you pick up the check!

➡ **L'Affable**
10, rue de Saint-Simon, 75007
Phone: 01 42 22 01 60
M° Rue-du-Bac
www.laffable-restaurant.fr

Closed on Saturday and Sunday

● Lunch set menu for 28€
● Dinner for about 60€

LA FERME SAINT-SIMON

Saint-Germain – €€€€ | Private room available

Once upon a time, this place, opened by Denise Fabre (the most famous TV presenter in the 1970s) and her chef husband Francis Vandenhende, had every famous Parisians in the arts, literature, and television running to it. This joyful and carefree clientele has since given way to ambassadors and office-workers from the nearby ministries, as well as the neighborhood bourgeois, satisfied with this well-behaved home cooking. Consequently, the atmosphere is quiet with good manners, and conversations are had in a low voice. The regulars like the fact that the tables are well set apart; the décor, entirely re-done in a chic, contemporary style which mixes leather, copper, mirrors, and

woodwork (we love the ceiling lights); and the adjoining salons, where government secrets can be exchanged without fear.

The menu celebrates the usual bistro bourgeois cuisine: the organic egg is accompanied by boletus mushrooms; the guinea fowl is from the famous farm La Cour d'Armoise; the Bigorre pig flirts with a potato millefeuille, and the sweetbread is perfumed with Lautrec pink garlic purée. It is delicious, very refined, and quite original. The service is as good as in a three-star restaurant, which is always pleasant, even when you are presented with the check, and have to double-check the prices three times if you made the error of ordering outside the set menus.

➡ **La Ferme Saint Simon**
6, rue de Saint-Simon, 75007
Phone: 01 45 48 35 74
M° Rue du Bac
www.fermestsimon.com

Closed for lunch on Saturday and all day Sunday

● Lunch menus at 29€ and 35€
● Free choice between 70€ and 90€

AU BON ACCUEIL
Tour Eiffel – €€€€

This is a place that's still unheard of, but which has quietly and peacefully lived out its life since 1870 in the shade of the Eiffel Tower. In a large room with a bourgeois feel, underneath a large Impressionist painting where Japanese air stewardesses come regularly to breathe the Parisian air, you will find wisdom in the well-crafted dishes. They involve good market produce and vegetables from Joël Thiébault that are well prepared: poached squid served cold with radish, celery and lettuce garlic cream (wonderful); or roasted piglet, both crisp and melting with sautéed vegetables seasoned with Sichuan pepper.

Chef Keita Kitamura delivers a modernized, refined cuisine, in a setting that is just as well-behaved, where the service in black aprons delivers daily on the promise written in gold on the façade, *Au Bon Accueil*: a nice welcome.

➡ **Au Bon Accueil**
14, rue de Montessuy, 75007
Phone: 01 47 05 46 11
M° Alma-Marceau
www.aubonaccueilparis.com

Closed on Saturday and Sunday

● Menus for 35€ and 55€
● Free choice between 70€ and 80€

× **LA FERME SAINT-SIMON** ×

In this chic, contemporary setting, the menu showcases the usual bistro cuisine,
and there are small adjoining salons where secrets can be shared freely...

× **CHEZ MONSIEUR** ×
In this 1940s setting, the *blanquette* is served in a casserole,
and the crepes Suzette offer a good show when they go up in flames in front of guests.

BACHAUMONT

Montorgueil – €€€€ | Table d'hôtes – Terrace

There is no doubting the fact that the Experimental group has talent. After opening cocktail bars and obsessional restaurants (Beef and Fish Club), here they are in a chic bistro on the ground floor of the 1960s Art Deco hotel that electrifies Montorgueil: the Bachaumont.

This former clinic was remodeled with chic but not bling décor designed by Dorothée Meilichzon, to welcome homemade cuisine against the odds: the eggs mimosa will take you back to your childhood; the tender beef with shallots is juicy as ever; the roasted free-range chicken are well tanned, and the chocolate tart is intense. That's enough to attract a crowd of hedonists beneath the glass ceiling, with a view of the kitchen. They come here to satisfy their needs for beauty and good food. Even the coffee, prepared by a barista, displays talent, and can be tasted as early as breakfast time in the hotel. This is surely an address of good taste.

➡ **Bachaumont**
18, rue Bachaumont. 75002
Phone: 01 81 66 47 50
M° Sentier
www.hotelbachaumont.com/
fr/pages/Restaurant_&_bar

Open every day, until late

● Lunch menus at
24€ and 29€
●Free choice between
40€ and 50€

CHEZ MONSIEUR

Madeleine – €€€€ | Small Terrace

When it changed owners, the Royal Madeleine glossed over its façade to become Chez Monsieur. The 1940s décor, on the other hand, remained: the floors have the patina of generations of varnished shoes, and the quality of the service – in black and white – is still the same. On the walls of the two large rooms, copper and souvenirs; and the tables with white tablecloths are set apart by frosted glass to preserve intimacy. This is where the show happens: food is sliced, chopped, and flambéed in front of guests, to keep traditions alive. This is probably what the tourists who flock here from the nearby hotels like so much, as do the Parisian hedonists.

Martin Harispe's food is also greatly appreciated. He used to work with Yannick Alléno at Meurice, and cooks well-rounded bourgeois plates. Don't miss the deliciously creamy veal *blanquette* served in a casserole that you can also order to go; the infinitely delicate sea bass *meunière*; or the always renewed crepe Suzette

show, which bursts into flames in front of the customers. Note that a few tables are set on the sidewalk outside.

LE BISTRO VOLNAY

Place Vendôme – €€€€ | Micro-terrasse – Comptoir

When you come into this Art Deco bistro, whose décor has been faithfully restored by Philippe Marques – former sommelier for the Prince of Wales and owner of this place – you will be drawn to the classic retro chic, by the gilding, the frosted glass, the sculpted bar, and the perfectly set tables. In good company at the counter (there are two seats that all the regulars fight over), you will hear and share stories from another time. You may believe you're seeing Paul Morand in a corner, and you'll wish you could leave in a dreamy Bugatti that will be waiting for you out front. At Bistro Volnay, the setting will trigger your imagination, and folklore is eaten elegantly.

The pretty bourgeois cuisine allows itself a few cheeky departures under Thomas Moretto's freed talent (he stayed for six years at the George V prior to working here). The menu follows the seasons, and honors the classics with fresh market produce. The result: splendid plates, full of nostalgia, brought to you by a careful service and well-balanced by an inspired wine list. The roasted guinea fowl, poached foie gras, coastal cod and gruel risotto, crisp sweetbreads with leeks carbonara... It's as though the menu is listing our own personal desires. Don't miss the veal and jumbo shrimp tartar, made according to Alain Senderens' recipe, along with the citrus rum baba, before jumping into your Bugatti.

➡ **Chez Monsieur (Royal Madeleine)**
11, rue du Chevalier-de-Saint-George, 75008
Phone: 01 42 60 14 36
M° Madeleine or Concorde
www.chezmonsieur.fr

Open every day

● Free choice around 60€

➡ **Le Bistro Volnay**
8, rue Volney, 75002
Phone: 01 42 61 06 65
M° Madeleine

Closed on Saturday and Sunday

● Menus for 34€, 38€ and 65€
● Free choice around 45€

THE *PATRON:* THE SOUL OF A BISTRO

The chef. He's all we ever talk about. We even spell his name with a capital. Sir, yes, Sir! Overexposed, he is envied and given constant attention, he is treated like a rock star and the foodistas – who can't tell the difference between a red mullet and a sea bass – are the backstage groupies. He is the new hero of gastronomy, the alpha. And yet...

How can we forget the person who lurks in the shadows of the media, but walks around in plain sight in the dining rooms of an animated bistro, making it the success that it is? We must render unto Caesar what is Raimu's, because he's the real boss, the pillar on which our appetites can depend, and the *joie de vivre* of the restaurant.

Just look at him welcoming the customers and calling them by their first names! He is never short of a kind word or an anecdote. Watch him as he orchestrates the ballet of the wait staff, giving them their roles and the plates as they pass over the threshold of the kitchens. See him noting the orders down, commenting on the chalkboard like you would read an Audiard, describing the wines with flowery discourse.

In some secret places, the wonderful tradition of family service is still alive, where the husband cooks and the wife takes care of the rest. The *patron* is the *patronne*: welcoming, she is every customer's mom at every service, care-giving and friendly, with a perfect knowledge of the menu... She's also the reason we come three times a week to sit at the table of the same neighborhood bistro.

Some say that the breed is in danger of extinction. Maybe it is. But that's all the more reason to show them our infinite gourmet gratitude.

* French actor Raimu played César Ollivier, the owner of the famous Bar de la Marine, in a 1931 rendition of Marcel Pagnol's trilogy, set in Marseille.

LAZARE

Saint-Lazare – €€€€

When a Michelin-starred chef takes his pans to the middle of a train station, everyone hears about it. Eric Fréchon (who won three stars for the Bristol) heads this chic and contemporary bistro that transmits a family vibe in a wonderful setting, with white dishes and bottles on the walls.

He offers a sepia-tinted version of bourgeois gastronomy (with an old-school weekly menu: quenelles on Mondays, calves' liver on Tuesdays), but it is painted in modern shades: the sea-food platter serves jellied whelks and the Mirabelle plums are pan-fried and seasoned with verbena. The bill will be as high as you want: the cream mussels cost 16€ and the veal 35€ – the prices have a wide span. The clientele is made up of travelers during the day and Parisian locals at night.

➡ Lazare
Saint-Lazare station forecourt, rue intérieure, 75008
Phone: 01 44 90 80 80
M° Saint-Lazare
www.lazare-paris.fr

Open every day

● Daily special at 18€
● Grandma's lunch on Sunday for 38€
● Free choice between 30€ and 50€

CHEZ GÉRAUD

Passy-La Muette – €€€€

Géraud Rongier, the troublemaking bistro-owner of La Muette, has stepped down but he left the décor of his charming restaurant with its bourgeois comforts intact. There is a large, luminous room with ribbed armchairs, heavy tablecloths, and family silverware: we're in the 16th all right. At the end of the room, though, a very beautiful wall mosaic from Sarreguemines gives this chic neighborhood bistro a hint of Montmartre mischief.

The duo who took over in the main room and the kitchen have valuable experience in the most prestigious houses (many years with Ducasse before working at the Royal Monceau). They create nice yet sharp plates that convey tradition without being boring. The cod with caviar and spinach is draped with beurre blanc sauce of surprising vivacity; the poached poultry is dressed in a crisp skin; and the rum baba is soaked on the spot, bottle in hand. Nice white Burgundy wines accompany the food. The neighborhood clientele loosen their ties a little as evening falls.

➡ Chez Géraud
31, rue Vital, 75016
Phone: 01 45 20 33 00
M° La Muette
www.chezgeraud.com

Closed for lunch on Saturday, and all day Sunday

● Lunch set menus for 29€ and 35€
● Free choice between 50€ and 60€

CLOVER

Saint-Germain-des-Prés – €€€€

Is this a bistro or not? It's hard to tell... Let's set aside for a second the fact that the food here is inspired by a starred chef, Jean-François Piège (Le Grand Restaurant), and let's take a look at this place: the room is a corridor with a well-equipped kitchen whose luxurious and bright stainless steel faces the unclothed tables; the décor and materials have clearly been chosen carefully (Japanese terracotta on the walls, mosaic woodwork, clear seats nicely hemstitched). The peacefulness of this place is barely disturbed by the fact that it is so small, the tables so close together and the noise levels so high.

What about the food? It's heartwarming, and novel. You are just as likely to find here a homemade dried sausage as a chicken broth infused with raw Jerusalem artichoke. You can eat the scallops with beetroot coulis with your hands (it's a must-eat: they are cooked on Parisian cobblestones heated in the oven); discover the round suavity with bitter flashes of a *foie pas gras* with passion fruit (it's the liver of the duck before it got force-fed); dissect the varied flavors of a young goat cooked different ways; and end with a roasted vanilla butternut with delicate straw-like aromas and an only slightly sugary taste. We'll call this place a "neo-bistro".

To top it all, the smiley service is impeccable, and the lunch menu is priced at 28€ (a blessing): it's worth the detour through Saint-Germain-des-Prés. Make sure you book, of course: it can only seat 22 people, and fills up quickly!

➡ **Clover**
5, rue Perronet, 75007
Phone: 01 75 50 00 05
Mᵒ Saint-Germain-des-Prés
www.clover-paris.com

Closed on Sunday and Monday

● Lunch menus at 28€ and 42€
● Dinner menus at 58€ and 73€

× **LAZARE** ×

This place, with white porcelain and bottles on the walls, is for every budget, and every taste:
the whelk shares the menu with beef, Mirabelle plums, and verbena.

× **CLOVER** ×
Japanese terracotta on the walls, mosaic woodwork, and a bright, open kitchen:
in this peaceful setting, you will enjoy heartwarming and novel food.

Aymeric Mantoux's
VIEW ON BISTROS
—◆—
Journalist

"The next time I hear the word 'bistro', I'm getting my gun out", some people say. It has to be said that the first bistro I ever set foot in was a "Roman bistro" that had no hint of a bistro, and nothing Roman about it at all! My grandma, who was only interested in food for the soul and payed little attention to actual food, had the nasty habit of asking me to meet her there.

Come to think of it, the only thing that authentic bistros and their ugly doubles have in common is the lack of friendliness of the owners and wait staff. Yet it's been a while since ill-mannered soldiers came in there howling to be served. The tradition goes on still, and has become an excuse for the owners of such places to mistreat their clients. We love these places still, or at least we pretend to love them because, let's face it, us Parisians don't really love anything. And they have evolved quite a bit: the retro became neo, traditions turned into gastronomy. The pages of the guide you are currently holding in your hands are filled with the best addresses. Even Alléno has his own bistro Place de la Bourse – that's a symbol. And it's very good, too. A real chef's bistro: local food, playful charm, and lively. After all, even British pubs managed to modernize well. What's that saying again? The British fired the first shot?

DOWN
THE BLOCK

We love these. Every person has their own favorite, which they adore and protect, and whose name they whisper to their friends like a secret: "You'll see, the owner is great, and they cook ox cheek like no one else." These places are always there, always handy. Feeling blue? Come drown your sorrow in the weekly evening hullabaloo, and in shepherd's pie. An impromptu visit? Call and book, then go around the corner to celebrate the reunion with carbs. Back from a weekend and nothing in the fridge? Feeling suddenly lazy in front of the frying pans? All of these are valid reasons to flee there.

This is also the work bistro. The one that's a few blocks from the photocopying machine, where you go in a large group when the mood is up, on Fridays, or in hiding, when you don't feel like sharing lunch with your co-workers in the workplace.

We don't go there for the spectacular food, but for the happiness brought to us by an authentic place where the dishes don't disappoint, where the aromas convey a heartwarming ambiance with a family feel. In truth, what we look for there are our own habits. A ritual. A daily setting.

So we wouldn't travel across Paris to eat there, but when you're in the neighborhood, these are the places you should go.

LES ROUTIERS

Marx Dormoy – €€€€ | Corner bistro

This is a corner bistro of a kind that no longer exists: an authentic truck stop where you can go shamelessly to warm your heart and your stomach. Contrary to what the exterior may suggest, the décor inside has personality: an old bar that has had a full life, twentieth century posters, and regulars that come eat and drink underneath the boss's friendly gaze – as they have been doing for forty-five years.

The daily menu is informal and comes with no fuss: escargots, *andouille* from Vire, rillettes, veal escalope Normandy style, Provencal veal kidneys, steak with fries, mustard rabbit, cheese platter, red wine pitcher, and grandma's desserts. Chose whatever you feel like: it's all good and homemade. To top it all, the portions are gigantic. With such quantity and quality, the bill is very reasonable (around 30€) for a menu. At Les Routiers, the manners aren't refined, but who cares: here, you don't eat, you feast. Brassens, whose portrait is on the wall, would agree with us.

➡️ **Les Routiers**
50 *bis*, rue Marx-Dormoy, 75018
Phone: 01 46 07 93 80
M° Marx-Dormoy
or La Chapelle
www.restaurant-les-routiers.fr

Closed on Sunday

● Daily menu at 30€
● Free choice between 20€ and 40€

LE BAR FLEURI

Buttes Chaumont – €€€€ | Terrace

This is a real corner bistro: so Parisian, so popular. It's hidden on a quiet corner between Buttes-Chaumont and Jourdain, and it's been a wonder to passersby, people who work nearby, old people living in the neighborhood, workers, and students for decades now. Nothing has changed since then, either. The décor is still rather unlikely: it's made up of a nice bric-a-brac (a vintage gas pump, stuffed chickens, skis, lace drapes, typewriters, an old pipe, dried flowers...). And the cook is still the same, always there to send out little traditional dishes at lunch and dinner time.

These plates are not pretentious; they are good and they are cheap (the price is set to the dime). The roasted chicken (with homemade fries) at 6.86€ is probably the cheapest in Paris, eggs mayonnaise cost 2.95€, potatoes and herrings *à l'huile* is 4.95€ and quite good, and the desserts between 3.55 and 5.05€ provide skeleton service. It's nice to have a place like

➡️ **Le Bar fleuri**
1, rue du Plateau, 75019
Phone: 01 42 08 13 38
M° Botzaris or Buttes-Chaumont

Closed on Sunday

● Free choice around 15€

that, capable of feeding you without robbing you, in happiness and simplicity. We'd all feel better if we had a place like that down the block. It's great for an uplifting end-of-the-month meal, a cheap coffee (1€ at the counter), or a small beer with charcuterie (served all day).

CAFÉ TRAMA

Sèvres-Babylone – €€€€ | Tiny terrace

Two steps from Bon Marché, Marion Trama reigns over this pretty café-bistro, sharp as a Thiers blade. The decoration is 1950s inspired, with retro tiles, a marble counter, and vintage furniture.

The huge chalkboard goes straight to the point when it comes to pleasing customers: eggs mayo, organic and excellent; calf's head with gribiche sauce as an appetizer or in a light version (how smart!); a tartar from Desnoyer hand-prepared with a knife; an incredible croque-monsieur with truffle salt... The classics are made from good produce, and are smart, savory and very well presented on the plate.

On this street, there's no need to fuss. For a terrace lunch or a fiesta dinner, this is the place to go. The wines are sometimes natural, always well chosen. All in all, a precise and efficient bistro with a nice charm and comfy atmosphere. After all, the boss comes from a family of gourmets (her uncle runs a two-macaron restaurant). The prices are good, in an otherwise expensive neighborhood.

➡ **Café Trama**
83, rue du Cherche-Midi, 75006
Phone: 01 45 48 33 71
M° Vaneau

Closed on Sunday and Monday

● Free choice for around 35€

LE PETIT CÉLESTIN

Île Saint-Louis – €€€€ | Terrace

This is a real Parisian bistro! Its timeless décor is so typical, and so is its tiny kitchen, moleskin banquettes, ancient tiles, red Formica tables, checkered napkins, and daily papers. It is so generous, with nicely prepared dishes and good produce.

The food is savory but not clumsy, the chalkboard is filled with characterful dishes (oxtail pâté, sirloin steak from Salers, pig ribs from the southwest); nice meat and fish, homemade desserts, and seasonal vegetables. It is direct, with disheveled charm, good advice, and Parisian composure.

It's so frivolous: the tables are set on to the street, the terrace bathes in the sun and the colored paper lanterns face the Seine, giving the place the air of a dance hall. It's so lively, with a cosmopolitan clientele that has good appetite and contagious friendliness. You won't find hipsters here, but true hedonists. Go there when the sun is out, and with a light mood, to fully enjoy the wine list.

➡ **Le Petit Célestin**
12, quai des Célestins, 75004
Phone: 01 42 72 20 81
Mᵒ Sully-Morland
www.lepetitcelestin.fr

Open every day

● Free choice between 30€ and 50€

GOÛPIL

Pereire – €€€€ | Terrace

The number of regulars who rush to this beautiful bistro by the border of the 17th arrondissement, close to the Paris walls, is a clear indication of its quality. All the gourmets of this bourgeois neighborhood meet up here, happy to have found a place close to home to satisfy their appetite for the great classics.

In a clean, spacious, and wonderfully arranged room, the great dishes of French gastronomy are all on the menu. It changes each season, but the essentials are always here: eggs mayonnaise, porterhouse steak with pepper sauce, sea bass, roasted pork, floating islands, and, when available, real Caen tripe, prepared in a manner beyond reproach. If you love tradition and variety meats, go! The produce served is high quality, the portions are large, the sides are good, and the wine list is classic and serious. The service, in black and white, goes well with the food and the setting while bringing it warmth and a nice retro feel. As soon as the

sun comes out, you can enjoy all of this out on the terrace.

LE CETTE

Montparnasse – €€€€ | Small terrace

Louis Aragon and Elsa Triolet, Chaïm Soutine, Man Ray, Eugène Atget, Rainer Maria Rilke... They've all been on this street. In the final scene of *Breathless*, Jean-Paul Belmondo even collapses there. Today, it's the bistro Le Cette that's drawing all the attention in this famous street. Under the owner Xavier Bousquet's influence, the bistro became modern, elegant, and luminous. White on the walls, wooden seats and chairs, round ceiling lights. The clientele is literary and almost spiritual, as if to uphold the history of this connecting street that links boulevard Montparnasse to boulevard Raspail. It is also well suited to the food of the young Japanese chef (who trained at L'Ourcine), Katsunori Nakanishi.

In each and every plate he sends out, you can read his love for French culinary tradition. Tradition, dexterity, and creativity: that's a winning combination! We particularly want to mention his vegetables – never have they been so well treated – the wine list and the tiny terrace, which is perfect for sunny days. For lunch, the menu made up of simple dishes (scrambled eggs, braised pork, cod...) is a godsend. Do keep in mind, though, that this place is best suited to delicate appetites, rather than to big eaters.

➡ **Goûpil**
4, rue Claude-Debussy, 75017
Phone: 01 45 74 83 25
M° Porte de Champerret

Closed on Saturday and Sunday

● Free choice around 40€

➡ **Le Cette**
7, rue Campagne-Première, 75014
Phone: 01 43 21 05 47
M° Raspail

Closed on Saturday and Sunday

● Lunch set menu between 18€ and 22€
● For dinner, free choice between 50€ and 60€

× **LE PETIT CÉLESTIN** ×
This place may look like a dance hall, but it certainly serves food with character.
This is a true Parisian bistro, with moleskin banquettes and checkered napkins.

LE BON SAINT POURÇAIN

Saint-Sulpice – €€€€ | Small terrace

There aren't many bistros that successfully revive the left bank spirit. This one hasn't changed its name, which evokes wine-producing regions and vacations, but it did redecorate and brighten the colors of its bourgeois cuisine. And that's what we love. This address close to Saint-Sulpice, then, has new décor, and it throws the deep blue reflection of its façade onto the street, where a few Baumann Scandinavian chairs are laid out. The neighborhood clientele is delighted with this godsend of a place, which offers them a tiny (so tiny) but bright room with clean yet relaxed tables.

In the kitchens, Mathieu Techer (formerly at Senderens) was given the reigns: he is serious and gifted, and gives a few traditional dishes (the menu is tiny too) nice contemporary highlights. The leeks vinaigrette with soft-boiled egg screams freshness, his roasted veal with green asparagus is crisp and cooked to perfection, and his rum baba hides pineapple underneath its light vanilla foam. The food is just like the décor: fresh, clear, and lively. It is delicious, joyous, and well-made and, although it's a little expensive (there are no sets nor special menus), we love it still...

➤ **Le Bon Saint Pourçain**
10 *bis*, rue Servandoni,
75006
Phone: 01 42 01 78 24
Mᵒ Saint-Sulpice

Closed on Sunday and Monday

● Free choice between 40€ and 50€

LE BOUGAINVILLE

Bourse – €€€€ | Terrace – Large tables – Sandwiches

In the sumptuous Vivienne gallery, Le Bougainville is a laid-back place; a large family restaurant with a long terrace. The décor isn't particularly original, there is nothing particularly memorable about it besides the 1950s bar and the ancient tiles: Formica banquettes surround Formica tables covered with paper tablecloths. But who cares! The eclectic clientele is a nice, rare mixture of middle-class and bourgeois, and they don't come here for the setting.

➤ **Le Bougainville**
5, rue de la Banque, 75002
Phone: 01 42 60 05 19
Mᵒ Bourse

Closed on Monday nights and Sunday

● Set lunch menu for 17.50€
● Free choice around 30€
● Sandwiches between 4€ and 6€

The atmosphere seems out of time, and you will enjoy great wines with honest little dishes that are both modest and well-prepared. The eggs mayonnaise are served according to gourmet tradition, the lard andouille is generous, meats are devil-may-care (beef, mustard andouillette, filet of duck breast...), homemade fries are beautiful, and cheeses are excellent. The lunch set menu that offers all of this should put you in a good mood. And if that's not the case, we count on the traditional-style service to make that right!

LE 6 PAUL BERT

Faidherbe-Chaligny – €€€€

After opening Le Bistrot Paul Bert (a solid Parisian bistro) and L'Écailler du bistrot (which specializes in shellfish), Bernard Auboyneau wanted to do something a little lighter. The result is this place, a modernized bistro.

The sauces and jaunty dishes are out: here, the work of adapting classics is done with delicacy. Vegetables play a leading role in these explorations, and taste comes first. The tartar is served between land and sea, with veal, shells, and herbs. Scallops are lightly roasted with parsley and lemon, and the quail is served with beetroot purée and a bouquet of vinegared carrots.

The 19€ lunch set is a godsend, even if the portions aren't really big enough to satisfy large appetites. In the evening, the prices rise quickly, with a 44€ menu, but the sophistication of the food follows suit. The wine list is audacious and pairs well with the food. We raise our glass to the Japanese chef Kosuke Tada, who brings a real and joy-provoking modernity to the classical yet pretty décor (red banquettes, counter, and window filled with traditional ingredients).

➡ **6 Paul Bert**
6, rue Paul-Bert, 75011
Phone: 01 43 79 14 32
M° Faidherbe-Chaligny

Closed for lunch on Tuesday and all day Sunday and Monday

● Lunch set menu at 19€
● Dinner menu at 44€
● Free choice around 50€

× **LE 6 PAUL BERT** ×

The sauces and jaunty dishes are out: here, vegetables play a leading role,
the chef creates and reinvents classics in an authentically modern décor.

LE GARDE TEMPS

Pigalle – €€€€

The façade is discreet, but don't judge a book by its cover! Inside this restaurant with bistro charm, which looks like a New-York building with its brick walls, the noise increases as the plates go by and the bottles (very well chosen by the *patron*, Marc Rosenzweig) are emptied. In such cacophony, it might be hard to whisper sweet nothings in your lover's ears. But to hell with romance! People come here to sit between walls decorated with black-and-white photographs, and to treat themselves without simpering.

The chalkboard changes every three weeks, and reveals southwestern bistronomy accents with a skillful mixture of tradition and new inspiration orchestrated by a former student of Yves Camdeborde. For instance, try the seasonal vegetable *pot-au-feu* with horseradish foam, or the roasted ray with hay butter and pumpkin purée. The produce is of good quality, and the cooking careful and generous. The prices are good, and should allow you to choose a nice wine (the wine list gets a little expensive) without ruining yourself.

➡ **Le Garde Temps**
19 *bis*, rue Pierre-Fontaine, 75009
Phone: 09 77 40 34 13
M° Blanche, Pigalle
or Saint-Georges
www.restaurant-legardetemps.fr

Closed on Sunday and for lunch on Saturday

● Set lunch menu between 17€ and 23€
● For dinner, free choice for about 40€

CAFÉ DES MUSÉES

Marais – €€€€

This is a cafe in name only! It is a true bistro of the best kind, welcoming during rush hour (which is practically all the time). Its timeless décor (with mosaics on the floor and old-school posters) and lack of tablecloths impresses gourmet tourists and crafty Parisians alike. It is noisy, but we'll consider that part of the charm.

In the solid and nicely turned-out kitchen, the classic repertoire is well balanced and sways between a Calvados poultry pâté and a seasonal vegetable cocotte with olive oil; between pork knuckle cooked in beer and yellow onions and cottage cheese with Jura-honey. The vegetables are very well prepared, which is rare enough in the bistro world to be noted. You can eat at the bar in front of the endless stream of plates, and with nice smells coming from the kitchen. The wine list is as solid as the customers' appetites, with a glass of Drappier champagne for 8€ to start off your meal.

LES POULETTES BATIGNOLLES

Batignolles – €€€€

Behind a recently revamped (and rather chic) façade, you will find peace in this L-shaped room with matt blue lights – a neo-bistro which serves sincere food, and treats north Parisians with big appetites to good calories. The décor includes a zinc bar with huge chalkboards, dark wood, and laid-back tables, free of tablecloths at lunchtime.

On the plate, you will recognize chef Ludovic Dubois' influences: his French masters (among whom Michel Rostang) and his Catalan past (he spent more than 10 years in Barcelona). The eggs are served studded with pata negra, artichokes, and tartar sauce with a delightful, gentle warmth. We mentioned Spain, which means chorizo, discreetly added to an iconic dish that mixes pig with perfectly pan-fried squid.

A little piece of advice: try some of the Spanish wines which Judith Cercós, a true Iberian and former sommelier at the Mandarin in Barcelona, picked out. They are perfect companions (or counterparts) to the well-flavored cuisine, rich (very rich, be warned), and well balanced. Just what we love!

➡ Café des Musées
49, rue de Turenne, 75003
Phone: 01 42 72 96 17
M° Chemin-Vert
www.lecafedesmusees.fr

Open every day

● Set lunch menu for 17€, dinner set menu for 27€
● Free choice between 35€ and 45€

➡ Les Poulettes Batignolles
10, rue de Chéroy, 75017
Phone: 01 42 93 10 11
M° Rome or Villiers
www.lespoulettes-batignolles.fr

Closed on Sunday and Monday

● Free choice between 40€ and 50€

LE JAJA

Île de la Cité – €€€€ | Small terrace – Nice wine cellar

This good address, hidden at the end of a small court-yard in the Marais, got a lot of attention at some point, and we'd be wrong to forget it, because this modern bistro with nice, luminous décor is filled with delights.

In the kitchen, the Italian chef works with excellent produce to compose dishes that convey both simple and sophisticated flavors (it's possible). The inspiration follows the seasons and is constantly renewed. Here, there is wide knowledge when it comes to drinks, and the wine list is filled with good suggestions, both natural and not, always well chosen and at every price point.

The wait staff are young, but devoted to ensuring that customers have a great time. When the sun is out, you can eat on the terrace or on the verandah, and taste the sweet Cévennes onion soup or the Venetian cod – having a great time here is not very difficult.

➡ **Le Jaja**
3, rue Sainte-Croix-de-la-Bretonnerie, 75004
Phone: 01 42 74 71 52
M° Hôtel-de-Ville
jaja-resto.com

Open every day

● Set lunch menu between 15€ and 23€
● Free choice between 40€ and 60€

MAKOTO AOKI

Champs-Élysées – €€€€

Japanese chefs are not quite done in declaring their love to French bistros. When heading up Parisian kitchens, they revisit iconic recipes with refinement. The plates are all the subtler, even if they do sometimes lose a bit of their original generosity. Makoto Aori is a little less stripped-down than other Japanese chefs, and he proposes bistronomy food full of tradition and surprises.

➡ **Makoto Aoki**
19, rue Jean-Mermoz, 75008
Phone: 01 43 59 29 24
M° Saint-Philippe-du-Roule

Closed on Sunday

● Set lunch menu for 23€
● Dinner menu for 38€
● Free choice around 50€

The façade says his name in white letters, but the food isn't Japanese at all. Of course, the dishes have exotic influences: the red wine kidney is accompanied by fruit; the filet of duck breast is served lacquered. But the menu, subtitled in Japanese for his numerous fellow countrymen, offers a rejoicing list of classics cooked with vigor and skill. Whether you choose the mussel soup, the morel brioche, or the Aubrac beef with mashed potatoes, you won't be disappointed by the talent and the precision displayed by this chef, who trained with the best. A delicate bistro, with efficient and discreet service, and good prices for lunch.

LA RALLONGE

Mairie du xviiiᵉ – €€€€ | Counter – Nice wines

Rallonge means "extension" in French, and that's just what this is. Talented chef Geoffroy Maillard extended his Table d'Eugène (one Michel star) to the top of rue Eugène-Sue, to create a true annexe. This is where people who enjoy gourmet cuisine and friendly wines come, every night, in the noisy and disheveled ambiance that only bistros can create.

They treat themselves to seasonal dishes served in modest portions – to encourage sharing and discoveries – and drown them with honest wines, kindly priced. When the weather gets cold, you will find comfort in the now-iconic and wickedly unctuous pasta shell risotto with boletus and truffles. If the weather clears, try the *chipirons à la plancha* with paella rice, Parmesan, and *piquillos*. Behind the counter, the service is always smiley. That's where we like to sit. Soon, it'll be your favorite spot too.

➡ **La Rallonge**
16, rue Eugène-Sue, 75018
Phone: 01 42 59 43 24
Mᵒ Jules-Joffrin or
Marcadet-Poissonniers
larallonge.fr

**Closed for lunch and
on Sunday**

● Small plates between
7€ and 14€
● Free choice between
30€ and 40€

× JAJA ×

Hidden at the end of a small Marais courtyard, this bistro with its nice, luminous décor is filled with delights, and the Italian chef's inspiration evolves with the seasons.

× **YARD** ×

Cider mussels, grilled honey carrot tempura... In this former ironwork studio, you will be drawn to the colors and the composition of your plate, before being won over by the tastes and smells.

YARD

Père-Lachaise – €€€€ | Small terrace

Shaun Kelly left the kitchens of this pretty bistro on rue de Mont-Louis a short time ago. But the beautiful Jane Drotter – a brilliant strategist – replaced her quickly with a chef who's just as impertinent and talented. Chez Yard, the British chef Nye Smith is now head chef. And the recipe hasn't changed: the same ingredients still ensure this small bistro's success.

The new arrival has even given this place a boost. The menu is short and seasonal, written every day on the chalkboard, and it uses quality produce to make inspired dishes, creative and savory (cider mussels, homemade duck ravioli, grilled honey carrot tempura...). You will be drawn to the colors and the composition of your plate, before being won over by the tastes and smells.

The service, managed by the owner, is still sunny and efficient. The building is a former ironwork studio, proud with a trendy British look. A small terrace is made up on the sidewalk during the summer. The lunch set menu is 18€, and it is amazing and generous, fresh and creative.

➡ **Yard**
6, rue de Mont-Louis, 75011
Phone: 01 40 09 70 30
M° Philippe-Auguste

Closed Monday evenings, and all day Saturday and Sunday

● Lunch set menu between 15€ and 18€
● Free choice around 30€

CAFÉ CONSTANT

Champ de Mars – €€€€ | Terrace

Christian Constant has made this street of the 7th arrondissement his kingdom. He owns four restaurants lined up along the same street, although all different. Between the luxurious restaurant, the shellfish restaurant, and the cocotte restaurant, there is this café, which the chef cooked up as a timeless bistro, an almost-perfect canteen. The décor is classic, with red banquettes, a large counter, and tiles on the floor. The result is classy, vintage, and laid-back.

The menu is flawless: you can pick your food on the chalkboard which features the current specials, directly inspired by the day's market. Appetizer, entrée, or dessert: in the recipes that this godfather of bistronomy (who used to head the Crillon kitchen) has allegedly stolen from his grandmother, it's all about tradition, generosity, and know-how. The wine list is just as appropriate.

The best thing about this place, though, is the check. The prices are fair, not to say kind, given the quality of the produce and the cooking. The lunch set menu is between 16€ and 23€, and the free choice amounts to about 40€. However, this place doesn't take bookings. So, to be sure you can get a table, you may need to get there very early. But what does it matter, if you're going to eat so well?

➡ Café Constant

139, rue Saint-Dominique, 75007
Phone: 01 47 53 73 34
M° La Tour-Maubourg
www.maisonconstant.com

Open every day

● Lunch set menu for 23€
● Free choice for about 40€

LAITERIE SAINTE-CLOTILDE

Rue du Bac – €€€€

In this neighborhood filled with ministries and old-school restaurants, this small, modern bistro is laid-back. Situated in an old dairy, the mood is bohemian rather than bourgeois! The checkered tablecloths have given way to mismatched Formica furniture, but the smiles are still here. The laid-back and sunny welcome sets the mood.

The menu is displayed on a chalkboard, and features two or three daily specials. There are well-made classics, taste, good produce, and fresh ideas. The food is sometimes nostalgic, and can sometimes be unexpected (*pot-au-feu* inspired by Chinese cuisine, roasted pig with shells...). The cooking is simple, but it's also smart. Meals proceed cheerfully, accompanied by wine (the wine list is short but inspired), and finishes well (cheesecake-lovers will be happy). And if all this is not enough, note that the check will be a pleasant surprise too!

➡ Laiterie Sainte-Clotilde

64, rue de Bellechasse, 75007
Phone: 01 45 51 74 61
M° Rue-du-Bac, Solférino
or Varenne

Closed for lunch on Saturday, and all day Sunday

● Lunch set menus between 21€ and 25€
● Dinner for about 35€

AMARANTE

Bastille – Gare de Lyon - €€€€

Some details don't lie. Take the *bon vivant* attitude of Amarante's chef Christophe Philippe, for instance. His gourmet look, his stomach large enough to conquer Paris, the way he speaks of the excellent origin of the produce he uses in his bistro, the *Cuisine française* sign carelessly placed in the window: everything here hints that we've come to a wonderful bistro. The walls haven't been roughened, though, and there is no vintage furniture: the simple, clean décor suggests something close to banality. The show is elsewhere: it's in the beautiful and precise cooking, and what cooking it is! Veal tongue carpaccio with a small and refined salad made from Annie Bertin produce; a delicate sole with *panisse* (fries made from chickpea flour, very rare in Paris); tripe nicely offset with olives, reclining on one of the best purées in Paris... All of this is available in a 22€ set lunch! We'll happily add a 5–6€ wine glass to that, selected by Mouloud Haddaden: maybe a Morgon de Foillard, or a Vézelay de Montant-Thoden. It's all good. The service is attentive, to top it all.

➡ **Amarante**
4, rue Biscornet, 75012
Phone: 09 50 80 93 80
M° Bastille

Closed on Wednesday and Thursday

● Lunch set menus at 19€ and 22€
● Free choice between 40€ and 50€

BISTROT BELLET

Faubourg Saint-Denis – €€€€ | Private room available

The rue du Faubourg-Saint-Denis is tired of being exposed to all the latest trends and whims, from the burger hot-dog to the Kurdish kebab. In the middle of this hyper-exotic mood, the Bistrot Bellet is an authentic, true Parisian bistro. As you walk through the door, you will feel at home: dark wood counter, open kitchen where a former chef from Café des Musées works, vintage tiles, tablecloth-free tables, dimmed lights in the evening for a delicate atmosphere... And you will be caught up in the warm mood created by the loud and joyous noises of the neighborhood oldies and passing hipsters.

The generous plates provide the ideal level of comfort: chicken fricassee with mushrooms and *vin jaune* served in a cocotte with unctuous cream; sinfully good country pâté, nicely perfumed; veal kidneys with sherry, served whole with a subtle gratin dauphinois. Solid and sincere bistro cuisine is no secret here at Bistrot Bellet. Be patient when the place is full – you may have to wait a bit between courses. Thankfully, people's kindness makes it all ok, and the boss himself (Nicolas Lacaze) is seen running around during rush hour. The only down side: on certain weekdays, they are only open in the evening.

LE CORNICHON

Denfert-Rochereau – €€€€

It doesn't matter if the name (which means "pickle") doesn't inspire you, nor the décor with its white walls, a huge picture of a pickle, and slightly-too-green banquettes. In this talented bistro, the food is good, and that's all that matters. Especially if you are in the area, looking for a place to eat and get comfort.

The menu changes every day: it's hard to say ahead of time what dishes you are likely to eat. What we can say is that the kitchen is directed by a young chef who trained at L'Ami Jean, who is careful when choosing produce, who knows how to use technique to serve creativity, how to be precise with textures, seasoning, and cooking, and is generous when dressing the plates. The prices look good on the chalkboard, but beware all the extras. Nothing to revolt for though, and no one's forcing you to add any extras.

➡ Bistrot Bellet
84, rue du Faubourg-Saint-Denis, 75010
Phone: 01 45 23 42 06
M° Château-d'Eau

Closed for lunch on Wednesday, Thursday and Saturday; all day Sunday and Monday

● Daily special for 14€
● Lunch set menus at 18€
● Menus for 32€ and 36€

➡ Le Cornichon
34, rue Gassendi, 75014
Phone: 01 43 20 40 19
M° Mouton-Duvernet, Pernety or Denfert-Rochereau
www.lecornichon.fr

Closed on Saturday and Sunday

● Unique menu at 35€

LA PULPERIA

Charonne – €€€€ | **Meat from Argentina**

The mood is more than happy here. It's a little loud, too, but that's the kind of noise we like to get caught up in. The Argentinian chef knows how to get people excited. In this bistro, which is much less good-mannered than it seems, the cooking is generous and flamboyant.

The menu changes nearly every morning: bistro classics (a wonderful sweetbread, melting and crisp; braised foie gras...) mix with South American specialties like *anticuchos* (marinated beef hearts), ceviche, or plancha calamari. Meat-eaters will be pleased by the wonderful beef and Iberian pork, chosen with precision and cooked with passion. Good wine, often natural and well bred, flows here without putting out the fire.

In the evening, the check tends to get a bit high (around 50€ per person). Impoverished carnivores had better come for lunch, to take advantage of the 18.50€ lunch set menu (a great deal).

➡ La Pulperia
11, rue Richard-Lenoir, 75011
Phone: 01 40 09 03 70
M° Charonne or Voltaire
lapulperiaparis.fr

Closed on Sunday

● Lunch set menu at 18.50€
● Free choice for about 50€

× **LA PULPERIA** ×

This bistro, run by an Argentinian chef, is much less well-behaved than it looks,
and bistro classics mix with South American specialties. A flamboyant cuisine!

EAT-IN
WINE CELLARS

Some may think it incidental – a nice addition to the plate, which is queen, constantly brought back to its role as a foil : "To go with the *paupiettes*, get me a little côtes glass!" But sometimes, what seems accessory takes over what seems essential, and the usual hierarchy is shattered. The bistro you go to for food then transforms into a place where the drinks are more important, where you will come to taste wines chosen by experts, and share moments of joy in the light euphoria produced by a nice bottle.

A few smart, joyous, and easy-going places have understood this, and offer passersby and regulars nice discoveries for which the food will be a good escort. We call these places "eat-in wine cellars", and we love meeting there with friends to empty a few glasses in the human warmth of the evening.

Great provenance, classified pedigree, organic, natural or ethical wines, all of the styles are represented in these temples to wine, where drinks flow with talent. You will find true wine-lovers there, and knowledgeable ones, although they don't mind receiving advice from people who are even knowledgeable and talented than they are. That's the kind of attitude we suggest you adopt.

So, whether you're red, white, or rosé, here are a few Dionysian temples where the wine won't ever disappoint. Cheers!

LE VERRE VOLÉ

Canal Saint-Martin – €€€€ | Terrace – Wine cellar

This small wine cellar by the banks of the canal Saint Martin has come a long way: it grew into a bistro, with a grocer, a wine merchant, and even an annexe for seafood. The original house continues as it used to, offering excellent regional and natural wines for every budget, and with delicious sides. Except that now the small snacks that once served as sides have evolved into superb, bistonomy-inspired dishes.

Now, the boss' selection (which you can trust blindly: 7€ with the right to drink it on the spot) goes with a sausage and homemade unctuous purée, or with a well-balanced ceviche. The menu evolves with time, but we're never disappointed. And the food is worthy of the wine. In this joyous and slightly messy décor, where you may end up eating very close to your neighbor (consider booking), you will get sweetly inebriated. Even the prices are inebriating (with a daily special around 15€).

➡ **Le Verre volé**
67, rue de Lancry, 75010
Phone: 01 48 03 17 34
M° Jacques-Bonsergent
leverrevole.fr

Open every day

● Daily special around 15€
● Free choice around 30€

LES QUILLES

Ménilmontant – €€€€ | Small terrace

In this Ménilmontant bistro, which serves amazing wine, you can come to enjoy a simple and sincere cuisine. In the large and luminous room, bottles are opened with verve. They only serve natural, organic, or sustainable wines that the young boss – an autodidact – picks up himself from small producers. The selection has character, and the man speaks of it with enthusiasm and intelligence. It would be a crime not to take his good advice. So much for the glass, but what about the fork? Simple things, but not simple-minded: these recipes appease hunger with finesse.

The daily menu on the chalkboard is small, but you can select wonderful, traditional produce, both from land and from the sea, arranged with taste in creative yet simple recipes. A few examples: pink radish and periwinkle, fresh sausage, leek, salsify and yellow carrots. At Les Quilles, nothing is pretentious: the place doesn't look like much, and the décor is authentic – there's no question of turning this place into a trendy bistro or a fake-vintage setting. Narcissistic hipsters might get thrown off-track here. As chefs and dishes forever posture nowadays, it's nice to find a truly authentic place, where the kindness and honesty are not masks. Even the check is nice here.

LES ROUQUINS

Denfert-Rochereau – €€€€ | Terrace

The 14th arrondissement is full of surprises for whoever wishes to explore it. This superb bar is hidden behind a shared frontage, with no particular signs out. Start off by drinking a wonderful glass from Richard Liogier's selection, which he puts together from the best vineyards, oftentimes from Languedoc. Of course, it would be hard to stop at this: one glass turns into two ("Garçon! One more please!")

Comfortably seated in this intimate, simple, and friendly décor, you will taste the delicious Iberian charcuterie. Finally, you'll decide to stay for a meal, and choose from the chalkboard: wonderful cold tapas (iconic octopus and *chipirones* salad), delicious bistro classics adapted according to the daily market (an incredible, knife-prepared beef tartar). In this happy setting, where you'll be surrounded by comrades whose pleasure is contagious, you'll keep drinking as you eat. And stay as late as possible, which can be late.

➡ **Les Quilles**
123, boulevard
de Ménilmontant, 75011
Phone: 01 47 00 03 66
M° Ménilmontant

**Closed on Sunday
and Monday**

● Lunch set menu
for 12.50€
● Dinner menu around 25€

➡ **Les Rouquins**
146, rue du Château, 75014
Phone: 01 45 39 78 99
M° Pernety

**Closed on Sunday
and Monday
Open until 2am**

● Free choice for about 35€

× LE VERRE VOLÉ ×

The food is worthy of the wine in this joyous and slightly messy setting on the canal Saint-Martin bank.
Regional wines are excellent and the dishes are inspired.

× **LES ROUQUINS** ×
This bistro, with a rather ordinary exterior, is full of surprises!
An unforgettable wine bar, with Iberian charcuterie, tapas, entrées, and contagious joy…

COINSTOT VINO

Grands Boulevards – €€€€ | Covered terrace

In a few years, the passage des Panoramas has become a haven for good food. Passage 53 is here, along with the Gyoza Bar, Caffè Stern, and, at the end, Coinstot Vino. Its neighbors are sometimes too well-behaved or completely pretentious, but this bistro is a daring upstart, with genius when it comes to encouraging good times.

This place is for knowledgeable drinkers: the natural, organic, or eco-sustainable wines are selected with incredible intuition. The choice is joyous, and the traditional plates are appealing. The rustic cooking style goes well with the setting – a true bric-à-brac of old posters and piled-up bottles (an old bicycle was even left in a corner). What will you pick to accompany your drink? Calves' liver, Iberian pork, lard-smoked andouille? That's unless you're feeling in a lighter mood, and are more likely to find what you want on the snack menu: high-quality charcuterie (our favorite), handmade tarama, homemade pâté, or smoked swordfish. So, what will it be: red or white?

➤ Coinstot Vino
25-26, passage des Panoramas, 75002
Phone: 01 44 82 08 54
M° Bourse or Grands-Boulevards
coinstot-vino.com

Closed for lunch on Saturday and all day Sunday

● Lunch set menu for 16€ and 18.50€
● Free choice around 30€

BISTROY... LES PAPILLES

Panthéon – €€€€ | Large tables – Rugby games

The frontage sets the right mood: yellow and a reference to its southwestern accent. In this neighborhood bistro full of life and warmth, people don't fuss. The décor is free from ornaments: an old bar, colored mosaic tiles, and large wine shelves on the walls.

The bistro offers good references to accompany large portions of food (the first bottle is around 30€, or bring your own for 7€). The menu is short but appealing: the plates are robust, inspired by daily markets, and keep the traditional spirit alive. Charcuterie, escargots with parsley, sweetbreads, divine purée... The hedonist crowd that comes here creates a cheerful atmosphere for lunch and dinner. Not to mention during rugby games: this place is a rugby embassy. A perfect place to regain strength in a neighborhood that sometimes lacks simplicity.

➤ Bistroy... Les Papilles
30, rue Gay-Lussac, 75005
Phone: 01 43 25 20 79
M° Cardinal-Lemoine or Place-Monge
www.lespapillesparis.fr

Closed on Sunday and Monday

● Lunch set menu at 28€
● Dinner menu for 35€

CAFÉ DE LA NOUVELLE MAIRIE

Panthéon – €€€€ | Terrace – Wine merchant

This pretty, modern, and wood-clad bistro has it all. It's an excellent wine bar with incredible choice, almost exclusively natural wines and bearded wait staff in t-shirts – never shy of advice or anecdotes.

It's also a simple bistro with a seasonal menu sometimes oriented towards Aveyron, displayed on a chalkboard. Chicken, burrata, Utah Beach oysters, poultry liver pâté with sundried tomatoes, ham and mushroom tart, sausage and lentil salad, rice pudding, cherry clafoutis... All these classics are well prepared, generous, and made with talent.

It's also a café where you can come get an espresso at 8am, on the beautiful terrace facing a small square. You can snack all day long on pâté, dried sausage, or sardines with local beer. To sum up, this is a true cornerstone in the neighborhood, managed with care and flexibility by a crowd of young, passion-driven individuals. It's a place where students from the Sorbonne, left bank intelligentsia, and well-behaved tourists hang out.

➡ **Café de la Nouvelle Mairie**
19, rue des Fossés-Saint-Jacques, 75005
Phone: 01 44 07 04 41
M° Place-Monge or Cardinal-Lemoine

Closed on Saturday and Sunday, aperitif-meal on Friday

● Free choice for about 35€

Clotilde Roux's
VIEW ON BISTROS
— ◆ —
Consultant and culinary author

In the bistro family, you'll find the traditional, the neo, the corner, the contemporary, the canteen... In this family, every taste is represented, every budget, and every occasion. In France, we like to label things, though, and the common thinking is that the traditional bistro that serves veal **blanquette**, potatoes and herrings *à l'huile*, and game pâté is for men. Real men who aren't afraid to tie their napkin around their necks and eat with their fingers.

Nowadays, girls are supposed to prefer quinoa salad with avocado tartines. Cliché? Well, let's throw those overboard and celebrate women who, like me, enjoy pig's feet, eggs mayo, and *pâté en croûte*. It is possible to wear pumps, red nail polish AND love to devour grilled *andouillette* with greasy, melting sautéed potatoes. Can kidneys and calves' head please a woman? Yes, they can. Would women satisfy this (guilty) pleasure every week? Perhaps not, let's be honest. But go ahead and ask a man to eat in a detox organic coffeeshop every week!

The bistro has the ability to offer a whole art of eating. It provides reassuring and comforting food. Therein lies its strength.

HEALTHY BISTROS

Is this the future? Organic, gluten-free, seeds, kale, and veggie burgers... are they to replace boeuf bourguignon and *pâté en croûte* in our children's bistros? Maybe not. But that's no excuse to ignore these new trends. We love them when the sun is out on a terrace. Want freshness? Lightness? These places will welcome you and delicately unveil new savors.

Small selection.

ROSE BAKERY

Pigalle – €€€€ | Brunch

This British woman is a pioneer of cool-organic in Paris, and already has four locations. Come for lunch, for a snack, or for Sunday brunch: you'll be happy. If you can't decide, try the salads on the counter, and the carrot cake – they're iconic!

➡ **Rose Bakery**
46, rue des Martyrs, 75009
Phone: 01 42 82 12 80
M° Pigalle or Saint-Georges
Three other addresses:
30, rue Debelleyme, 75003;
Bon Marché, 24, rue de Sèvres, 75007; and 10, boulevard de la Bastille, 75012

Closes at 6pm during the week, and 5:15pm on weekends

● 7€–20€ dishes
● Pastries for about 5€

BOB'S KITCHEN

Turbigo – €€€€ | To go

This is one of the pillars of Bob's galaxy! Just like in the other three locations, this offers quality coffee, organic produce, inspired recipes, vegetables, and cold-pressed juices, in a laid-back atmosphere.

➡ **Bob's Kitchen**
74, rue des Gravilliers, 75003
Phone: 09 52 55 11 66
M° Arts-et-Métiers
Two other addresses:
15, rue Lucien-Sampaix, 75010, and 12, esplanade Nathalie-Sarraute, 75018
www.bobsjuicebar.com

Closes at 3pm during the week, and 4pm on weekends

● 5€–10€ dishes
● Desserts and soups for about 4€

LE BICHAT

République – €€€€ | To go

Augustin Legrand is a fighter. By opening this organic and health bistro, he wants to fight junk food by proving it's possible to eat well for not much money, and without waste. The setting is modern and welcoming, with large tables to share. On the menu: soups, generous rice bowls, veggies, protein (eggs, fish, or meat), and nice desserts. You'll be full, but you'll still ask for more!

➡ **Le Bichat**
11, rue Bichat, 75010
Phone: 09 54 27 68 97
M° Goncourt
www.facebook.com/restolebichat

Open every day, all-day service

● Full menus around 12€

× **LE BICHAT** ×

In this modern, welcoming, organic, and healthy bistro, the boss intends to kill junk food and prove it's possible to eat well for not much money. You'll be full, but you'll still ask for more!

SOUL KITCHEN

Montmartre – €€€€ | Brunch

This canteen is comforting, small, and filled with good things. Excellent morning coffee, afternoon pastries, and a lunch set menu that presents seasonal produce with wit. We'd spend the whole day here!

➡ Soul Kitchen
33, rue Lamarck, 75018
Phone: 01 71 37 99 95
M° Lamarck-Caulaincourt
soulkitchenparis.fr

Closed every evening during the week, and all day Monday

● Lunch set menu for 13.50€ during the week, 15.50€ on weekends

HOBBES

Belleville – €€€€ | Terrace – Brunch

Two steps from Buttes-Chaumont, this canteen is as green as the neighboring park, and pleases vegetarians and gourmets with savory and healthy dishes. Beautiful produce and lots of ideas on your plate! In the afternoon, this peaceful and colorful place changes into a delicate tea-house.

➡ Hobbes
31, avenue Simon-Bolivar, 75019
Phone: 01 42 02 79 50
M° Pyrénées
hobbes.fr

Closed on Monday, and evenings on Tuesday, Wednesday and Sunday

● Entrée for 10€, desserts for 5€, brunch for 19€
● Thursday night menu for 21€

LE BAL CAFÉ

Rue des Batignolles – €€€€
Terrace – Brunch

The location is perfect: a terrace facing a square in a tiny street, and the fascinating aura of the Bal and its documentary photography exhibitions. To top it all, the cooks, who used to work at Rose Bakery, have great dishes on the menu, made from fresh produce and with well-made drinks!

➡ Le Bal Café
6, impasse de la Défense, 75018
Phone: 01 44 70 75 51
M° Place-de-Clichy
www.le-bal.fr/le-bal-cafe

Closed on Monday and Tuesday

● Set menu between 15€ and 24€
● Brunch for 25€

× **LE BAL CAFÉ** ×

A terrace facing a square, the fascinating aura of the Bal and its exhibitions,
nice plates, fresh produce, and well-made drinks! Everything is perfect at Bal Café.

BLACKBURN COFFEE

Faubourg Saint-Martin – €€€€

The Marzocco coffee machine is placed next to homemade pastries, in a warm Scandinavian décor. For lunch, the plates are simple, balanced, and gourmet. You can spend the afternoon there drinking fresh fruit juices and excellent coffee.

➡ Blackburn Coffee
52, rue du Faubourg-Saint-Martin, 75010
Phone: 01 42 41 73 31
M° Château-d'Eau or Jacques-Bonsergent
www.blackburn-paris.com

Closes at 6pm during the week, and 7pm on weekends

● 13€ set menu, about 4€ for coffee

THE BROKEN ARM

Turbigo – €€€€ | Terrace

The name honors Marcel Duchamp. This beautiful shop displays clothes, books, and objects, and has a remarkable coffee-shop which serves well-dressed customers with inspired and creative plates, made from the best produce.

➡ The Broken Arm
12, rue Perrée, 75003
Phone: 01 44 61 53 60
M° Temple
the-broken-arm.com

Closed on Sunday, and all day from 7pm

● Free choice: about 20€ for two courses.

CAFÉ PINSON

Magenta – €€€€ | Brunch – To go

This café, decorated in good taste, offers savory, vegetarian, organic, and gluten-free food in its three locations. Plenty of women go there for the soups, large choice of salads, detox juices, and nice pastries (for those who are allowed dessert).

➡ Café Pinson
58, rue du Faubourg-Poissonnière, 75010
Phone: 01 45 23 59 42
M° Poissonnière
www.cafepinson.fr
Two other addresses: 66, avenue des Champs-Élysées, 75008, and 6, rue du Forez, 75003

Closed Monday, Tuesday, Wednesday, and Sunday nights

● Set menus between 14.50€ and 17.50€
● Brunch for 25€

AU FOND DU JARDIN

Nation – €€€€ | Terrace

The name gives away the secret location! At the back of a bar-restaurant, in a large courtyard that looks like a dance hall, filled with plants and thrift-shop furniture. You'll eat veggie burgers, large salads, and nice little plates. When the sun is out, it's party time!

➡ **Au fond du jardin**
39, rue Pelleport, 75020
Phone: 01 43 64 81 35
M° Porte-de-Bagnolet

Closed on Monday and on Sunday evening

● About 12€ for a course

LABEL FERME

George V – €€€€ | To go

"Fast food, direct from producers": the concept is simple and fresh! In this tiny place with country-style décor, you'll pick the ingredients yourself to make up a sandwich or a salad. Don't miss out! They've all been selected from the producers and artisans whose portraits are on the wall.

➡ **Label Ferme**
30, rue Washington, 75008
Phone: 09 81 33 36 49
M° George-V
labelferme.fr
Two other addresses: 43, rue Le Peletier, 75009, and 146, rue Montmartre, 75002

Closed on Saturday and Sunday, and from 2:30pm during the week

● Menus for 10€ and 11€

CAUSSES

Pigalle – €€€€ | To go

These last few years, Pigalle has filled up with quality bistros, all young, lively, and street-wise. Causses is one of them. On one side, there is a grocer with carefully selected produce. On the other side, a remarkable salad and sandwich bar with daily specials. Go to the top of the class!

➡ **Causses**
55, rue Notre-Dame-de-Lorette, 75009
Phone: 01 53 16 10 10
M° Pigalle
www.causses.org

Closed on Sunday, and every day from 3:30pm

● Set menus between 8.50€ and 14€
● Free choice between 5€ and 12€

DÜO

République – €€€€ | Brunch

Brunch or an exhibition? Let's do both! This alternative place in Popincourt offers emerging artists' exhibitions, seasonal vegetarian dishes, and even a library! There is a set lunch, small snacks in the evening to nibble on with a good beer, and brunch on weekends.

➡ **Düo**
24, rue du Marché-Popincourt, 75011
Phone: 09 82 49 43 63
Mᵒ Parmentier
www.facebook.com/duolovesyou

Closed on Monday and Sunday evening

● Set menus between 15€ and 18€
● Brunch for 19€

BLOOM

Bastille – €€€€ | Brunch – Terrace

Close to the bustle of Place de la Bastille, this canteen, with its tiny terrace, is a calm, restful place. The menu consists of regional organic produce only, and it's inspired: goat-cheese salad, vegetarian lasagna, meatballs...) For the aperitif: good beer and local tapas!

➡ **Bloom**
25, rue de la Forge-Royale, 75011
Phone: 01 43 72 87 88
Mᵒ Faidherbe-Chaligny
bloom-restaurant.fr

Closed on Monday, and Tuesday and Sunday evenings

● Menu at 14.50€
● Brunch at 20€

LE PAVILLON DES CANAUX

La Villette – €€€€ | Terrace

Walls with graffiti, dollhouse décor, a terrace by the water, delicious coffee, and a seasonal canteen, gourmet and balanced platters... This place used to be reserved for lock-keepers, but it's now very trendy in North Paris young gourmet circles. And we can figure out why!

➡ **Le Pavillon des Canaux**
39, quai de la Loire, 75019
Phone: 01 73 71 82 90
Mᵒ Riquet or Laumière
www.pavillondescanaux.com

Open every day

● Dishes between 8€ and 10€
● Pastries for 5€

× **LE PAVILLON DES CANAUX** ×

In this place, which used to be reserved for lock-keepers, you'll be delighted to taste gourmet and well-balanced dishes on the terrace... with your feet in the water

CONTENTS

INDEX BY ARRONDISSEMENTS

MARTINI

IV
LICENCE
Loi du
24 Sept. 1941

RICARD
ANISETTE

© Éditions du Chêne – Hachette Livre, 2016
www.editionsduchene.fr

Editor: Valérie Tognali, assisted by Sandrine Rosenberg
Proofreading: Valérie Mettais and Karine Elsener
Artistic Director: Sabine Houplain, assisted by Élodie Palumbo and Julie Delzant
Layout: Mateo Baronnet
Cover: Zoo design
Photogravure: Quat'coul
English translation by Justine Granjard
Proofreading by Laura Gladwin for Cillero & de Motta
English layout by Vincent Lanceau

Published by Éditions du Chêne
(58 rue Jean Bleuzen, CS 70007, 92178 Vanves Cedex)
Printed in Spain by Estella Graficas
Copyright registration: April 2017
ISBN 978-2-81231-634-0
31/2618/4-01